WILDERNESS MEDICINE

by

WILLIAM W. FORGEY, M.D.

Dr. Forgey is a Trustee, Wilderness Education Association; a Fellow of the Explorer's Club; the Medical Director, Lake County Juvenile Center; Trustee, Alternative House for Youth of Gary, Indiana; formerly an emergency room physician and Director of Emergency Medicine Department of the Ross Clinic, Merrillville; and currently in private practice in Merrillville, Indiana. Prior to going to medical school he held the rank of Captain, Infantry, with over two years of service in the former Republic of Vietnam. He is a Member of the Wilderness Medical Association and Associate Member of the University Association for Emergency Medicine.

ICS BOOKS, INC.
Merrillville, Indiana

WILDERNESS MEDICINE

Copyright © 1987 by William W Forgey, M.D.

10 9 8 7 6 5 4

Printed in U.S.A.

Published by:
ICS Books, Inc.
One Tower Plaza
Merrillville, IN 46410

Dedicated to the Staff of the Eckerd Family Youth Alternatives. Based in Clearwater, Florida, but with camps along the entire eastern seaboard, this group of dedicated counselors follow an inspired program of experiential education using wilderness living and tripping to aid troubled youngsters and under-achievers.

Library of Congress Cataloging-in-Publication Data

Forgey, William W., 1942-
    Wilderness medicine.

    Bibliography: p.
    Includes index.
    1. Backpacking -- Accidents and injuries.
2. First aid in illness and injury. 3. Wilderness
survival. I. Title. [DNLM: 1. Expeditions -- popular
works. 2. First Aid -- popular works. 3. Hygiene --
popular works. 4. Travel -- popular works. WA 292 F721w]
RC88.9.H55F67   1987   616.02'52   87-29325
ISBN 0-934802-37-8

HOW TO USE THIS BOOK

OUCH!

That hurts! Now how do I take care of it? With these words of panic one needs a source of rapid and thorough help. Starting on page 139 you will find the *Instant Reference Clinical Index* that will lead you to the correct page in this book. This index is cross-referenced by anatomical location, symptom, procedure, and topic.

And with what shall I treat it? The ideal medical kit will have multifunctional components. An example would be a medication which would treat many problems. thus cutting the cost, weight, and bulk of the medical kit, while also simplifying the list of items that must be studied. This book discusses treatment from three view points. One is the first aid measures that must be taken. The second is the use of items that can be obtained without prescription. The third is treatment with prescription medical articles. Discussion of medical kits and descriptions of their components begins on page 3.

Read this book before you need it in the field. It has been designed especially for use in isolated circumstances, where a physician is not available, and from whence evacuation is not feasible. Since the first edition in 1979 there have been many changes, both due to improved technology in medicine, to the increased availability of many items without prescription, and to recommendations from users in the field.

And it has been those users in the field that have made this whole project so gratifying. Some have had such exceptional experiences that I have traveled out to meet them, such as the Pugsley family in British Columbia who lived two winters in total isolation in the Western Rockies. And there have been many others who have taken considerable personal time to relate their experiences and provide suggestions for future editions. Two young men who had spent 7 months in a remote area of Canada suggested adding a section on swallowing kerosene, a trapper from Manitoba wanted further description on wound appearance after initial treatment, Valerie Fons and Verlen Kruger called from their three year canoe trip to state they were tearing excess pages from their copy to lighten their load. The many suggestions for additions and deletions have been taken to heart and a new edition of *Wilderness Medicine* has been prepared to make your trips into the isolated back country, the safe trip that it should be.

William W. Forgey, M.D.
Merrillville, Indiana
September 1987

"In uncommon or complicated cases ... I again advise every man without delay to apply to a Physician that fears God."

— John Wesley
Primitive Physick
1755

PRE-TRIP MEDICAL TRAINING — Those contemplating medical/surgical responsibility for major expeditions, where one would not anticipate the capability of medical evacuation or availability of professional medical assistance, should familiarize themselves with every piece of equipment and the techniques required for their proper use prior to departure. As a rule, one should be able to find an outing club with a physician who is sympathetic to your requirements. Your family physician may not be a wilderness traveler, but he may be willing to advise on the techniques mentioned in this book. First aid courses are usually available in every community. If in doubt, contact your local Boy Scout Council, which should have knowledge of a physician with an outdoor lean. Probably the most valuable first aid course generally available is the "First Responder Course" established by the DOT. Valuable, but less useable for wilderness purposes, is the American Red Cross "Advanced First Aid."

Basic skills should certainly include a course in Cardio-pulmonary Resuscitation (CPR) and the general method of treating shock. In addition, it would behoove the group medic to have adequate knowledge of the following:

Signs, prevention and treatment of "thermal injury," to wit:
   Hypothermia
   Frostbite
   Burns
   Hyperthermia
Prevention and treatment of blisters (friction), abrasions and cuts
Prevention and treatment of animal bites, snake bites, scorpion bites
   and other zoogenic trauma peculiar to the area of anticipated
   operation.
Prevention and treatment of poison plant dermatitis
Properly acquiring and treating potable water; human waste disposal
Recognizing and treating High Altitude Illness
Immobilization splinting
When and how to evacuate
Medical treatment of anaphylaxis (shock from bee stings, etc.)

Although these subjects are discussed in this book, it should be stressed that CPR is certainly a skill that must be learned and practiced under supervision in order to be properly implemented during a time of need. It will be impractical to practice some of the skills discussed in this book, but there is no excuse for *everyone* not becoming CPR qualified.

PRE-TRIP PREPARATION — The pre-trip phase is the most critical part of your trip. Proper preparation makes for a successful and safe expedition.

Most trips are not able to take into account the psychology and social skills of participants, but if this is possible it can avoid stress and conflict that can make a dream project turn into a nightmare. I have found a ten day preparatory trip is generally enough to identify idiosyncrasies that might indicate incompatibility. The great outdoorsman Calvin Rutstrum once summed this problem up when he mentioned to me one day, "How do you tell a guy you hate his guts by the way he holds his fork?" It's simply amazing how personal habits and quirks can grate on you. In reviewing many successful relationships during stressful trips, I have come to the conclusion that the most favorable relationship is one of "respect" — it surpasses love, hate, fear or any other human emotional form of inter-action. If you truly respect a trip partner, you can tolerate mannerisms and faults that would otherwise be unacceptable.

Plan a time schedule that allows for weather as well as terrain. Many accidents in the bush come from having to take chances while running out of time, food, etc., and turning the expedition into a retreat. Proper pre-trip physical conditioning cannot be stressed too highly. While trying to survive exposure, a major factor is your ability to generate heat, which is directly related to your ability to produce work. This is achieved through physical conditioning as the limiting factor, not how much food one stuffs into one's face.

A proper pre-trip dental exam should be made well in advance of the trip, thus allowing adequate time for possible needed corrections.

The pre-trip physical should include attention to immunization schedules that vary, depending upon the region of the world to be visited (see Appendix A). As a minimum, each trip member should have a current tetanus booster.

Base line resting pulse rate, blood pressure and urinalysis should be determined for each member. Examination for a hernia should be performed on males. A prostate exam upon all men over forty and a Pap smear upon all women taking birth control pills or those over age of forty should have been performed within the previous year. Cardiac stress testing (treadmill) is not required in persons with no symptoms of chest pain.

An eye examination should have been obtained within the previous three years by everyone. For those over forty, I recommend an eye exam (including glaucoma check) within the previous year.

Evacuation planning must be considered during the expedition planning phase. Medical insurance needs, particularly if foreign travel is contemplated, must be addressed. And the assembly of the medical kit must be accomplished.

You're going to need some help. The more that you read on this subject and the more medical training that trip members receive, the better off everyone will be. I recommend that you review the list of medical books in Appendix B. A frequent lament that I hear from the field is the lack of a local physician who could help by writing prescriptions for an adequate expedition medical kit. It is for this reason that even the first edition of this book had an extensive non-prescription medical kit designed to handle most problems that one might encounter in the bush. A list of suppliers of the non-prescription medications and virtually all of the instruments and high tech bandaging material described in this book can be obtained from the publisher by writing to: ICS Books, Inc., Box 10102, Merrillville, IN 46411. I have personally tried to help each and everyone writing me for assistance in obtaining requisite prescription medications.

THE WILDERNESS EXPEDITION MEDICAL KIT — The ideal medical kit will have multifunctional components to reduce the cost, bulk, weight, and simplify usage. It should also be modular to allow an increasing depth of care by including the more sophisticated modules only if the potential risks of the trip, or reduced access to medical help, warrants their inclusion. Most injuries and conditions described in this book can be treated with very little in the way of kit components. But I have included here state of the art items that would provide ideal treatment aid. As this book has been written for those who may be isolated without ready access to professional medical care, the treatments discussed go beyond normal first aid. The kit which follows similarly goes beyond what would be considered a "first aid" kit. But the initial modules are indeed easily useable under first aid conditions.

The kit consists of 6 units, or modules. In order of discussion will be the Topical Bandaging Unit, Non-Rx Oral Medication Unit, Orthopedic Unit, Field Surgical Unit, Rx Oral/Topical Medication Unit, and the Rx Injectable Unit.

As a minimum, the Topical Bandaging Unit and Non-Rx Oral Medication Unit will generally fulfill the vast majority of emergency treatment requirements. The Field Surgical Unit and the prescription modules are designed for long term, and more advanced patient care. All items listed in the kit modules can be obtained without a prescription, except in the modules clearly marked "Rx."

In addition to the above, everyone should carry a new piece of emergency equipment called "The Extractor." This 4 oz plastic suction device is ideal for use in the first aid treatment of snake bite, puncture wounds, and venomous stings. It is far superior to the rubber suction cup snake bite kit. Note description of use on page 115. Additionally, consideration should be given to a dental kit. Several are commercially available through backpacking and outdoor outfitters. As a minimum, a small bottle of oil of cloves can serve as a topical toothache treatment, see page 38. A fever thermometer should be included on your trip. People wearing contact lenses should carry suction cup or rubber pincher device to aid in their removal. Consideration must be given to a stethoscope and blood pressure cuff, if you know how to use them. They are must items for Search and Rescue Units, but not for the usual wilderness expedition. Provide an adequate means of water purification as indicated on page 79.

WILDERNESS EXPEDITION MEDICAL KIT
Topical Bandaging Unit

Quantity	Item
2 pkgs	Coverstrip Closures 1/4" x 3" 3/pkg
1 pkg	Coverstrip Closures 1/2" x 4" 6/pkg
6	Tegaderm 2 3/8" x 2 3/4"
2	Spenco 2nd Skin 3" x 13"
2	Spenco Adhesive Knit Bandage 5" x 6"
15 pkg	Nu-Gauze, high absorbent, sterile, 2 ply, 3" x 3" pkg/2
3	Surgipad, Sterile, 8" x 10"
2	Elastomull, Sterile Roller Gauze, 4" x 162"
2	Elastomull, Sterile Roller Gauze, 2 1/2" x 162"
25	Coverlet Bandage Strips 1" x 3"
1	Tape, Waterproof 1" x 5 YD
1	Tape, Hypoallergenic 1/2" x 10 YD
1	Hydrocortisone Cream .5%, 1 oz tube
1	Triple Antibiotic Ointment, 1 oz tube
1	Hibiclens Surgical Scrub, 4 oz bottle
1	Dibucaine Ointment 1%, 1 oz tube
1	Yellow Oxide of Mercury Ophthalmic, 2%, 1/8 oz tube
1	Tetrahydrozoline Ophthalmic Drops, .05%, 15 ml bottle
1	Miconazole Cream, 2%, 1/2 oz tube
1	Over-pack Container for above

Coverstrip Closures — by Beiersdorf is the best wound closure tape system that can be obtained. They stick better than "Steri-strips." They can be removed and re-applied while trying to adjust the wound edges and still stick firmly — something that a steri-strip cannot do. These strips breathe and can be left on as long as necessary for the wound to heal, often without an outer covering. By far better than "butterfly" bandages, the latter can be substituted if cost and availability is a factor.

Tegaderm — by 3M Corp. This is the "Gore-tex" of bandaging. This thin coating will seal water out, yet let a wound remain visible and breathe. It should be applied to dry wounds, ie wounds that are not seeping fluid or blood. Ideal for covering cuts as the user can continue to immerse the wound in water while canoeing, working outside, etc, without contaminating the injury. Other similar products exist, but in my tests this brand sticks and breathes the best.

Spenco 2nd Skin — Truly a major advance in field medicine. This inert hydrogel consists of 96% water and 4% polycthylene oxide. It is used on wet, weeping wounds to absorb these fluids and protect the injury. This is a perfect cure and prevention for friction blisters. It revolutionized the field treatment of 1st, 2nd, and 3rd degree burns, as it can be applied to all three as a perfect sterile covering and for pain relief. This item should be in every medical kit. The ideal covering pad is the Spenco Adhesive Knit Bandage. If used in treating blisters, remove one outer covering of cellophane only from the 2nd Skin, cover with the Knit Bandaging, and occasionally dampen with clean water to maintain the hydrogel's hydration. It will last a lot longer that way when in short supply.

Nu-Gauze Pads — J&J Company has developed a gauze that is 2 ply yet it absorbs nearly 50% more fluid than conventional 12 ply gauze pads. This may not seem important until a rapidly bleeding wound needs care. For years J&J has made a "Nu-Gauze" strip packing dressing — the Nu-Gauze pads are a completely different material. They are a wonderful advance in gauze design.

Surgipad — An 8x10 sterile bandage for covering or compression of large wounds. This bandage can be used as a feminine sanitary napkin. If this large bandage is not carried, then several Kotex or equal should be carried in every trip medical kit.

Elastomull Roller Gauze — A superior rolled gauze by Beiersdorf, it stretches, does not unravel, and has low dust content. Its sterile packages are ideal for field use. The gauze can be applied directly over wounds, or used to hold other bandaging material in position.

Coverlet Bandage Strips — Another Beiersdorf product. These are common 1"x3" bandage strips, but they are the best made. They stick even when wet, will last through days of hard usage, and stretch for compression on a wound or conform for better application.

Waterproof Tape — A tough tape that can be used for splinting or bandage application. No brand advantages that I can determine. A 1" by 5 yd roll on a metal spool is a useable size.

Hypoallergenic tape — A good size for attaching bandages to skin is 1/2" x 10 yds. Very light weight, made of paper or silk cloth. Many brands are suitable.

Hydrocortisone Cream .5% — 1 oz tube. This non-Rx steroid cream treats allergic skin rashes, such as those from poison ivy. A cream is ideal for treating weeping lesions, as opposed to dry scaly ones, but will work on either. To potentiate this medication apply an occlusive dressing (plastic cover) overnight.

Triple Antibiotic Ointment — 1 oz tube. Each gram of this ointment contains bacitracin 400 units, neomycin sulfate 5 mg and polymyxin B sulfate 5000 units. For use as a topical antibiotic in the prevention and treatment of minor infections of abrasions and burns. A light coat should be applied twice daily.

Hibiclens Surgical Scrub — This Stuart product [chlorhexidine gluconate 4%] far surpasses hexachlorophene and povidone-iodine scrub in its antiseptic action. Its onset and duration of action is much more impressive than either of those two products also.

Dibucaine Ointment 1% — 1 oz tube. This is a topical anesthetic agent which will very effectively numb the skin for temporary relief of pain and itching associated with sunburn, minor burns, insect bites and stings, and hemorrhoids. Apply 3 or 4 times daily.

Yellow Oxide of Mercury Ophthalmic 2% — 1/8 oz tube. Before the availability of prescription antibiotic eye medications, this was one of the best medications available for eye infections. It is the best non-Rx treatment currently obtainable.

Tetrahydrozoline Ophthalmic Drops .05% — 15 ml bottle. These eye drops are used for allergy relief and to remove red color and discomfort when due to smoke, eye strain, etc. It will not cure infection or cover the existence of a foreign body. Place 1 or 2 drops in each eye every 6 hours.

Miconazole Cream 2% — 1/2 oz tube. This is one of the most effective antifungal preparations available for foot, groin, or body fungal infections. Brand names are Monistat Derm and Miconazole. The former is sold by Rx only, but the generic product has been available without Rx since 1983.

WILDERNESS EXPEDITION MEDICAL KIT
Non-Rx Oral Medication Unit

Quantity	Item
24	Actifed Tablets (decongestant)
24	Mobigesic Tablets (pain, fever, inflammation)
24	Meclizine 25 mg tab (nausea, motion sickness prevention)
24	Benadryl 25 mg cap (antihistamine)
10	Bisacodyl 5 mg (constipation)
25	Diasorb (diarrhea)
25	Diulose (antacid)
6	1 oz Vials for repackaging the above
1	Over-pak Container for above

Actifed Tablets — Decongestant. Each tablet contains 60 mg of pseudoephedrine (a vasoconstrictor that dries up mucous formation) and 2.5 mg of triprolidine (an antihistamine to block allergic reactions). Normal dose is 1 tablet every 6 hours to relieve congestion in nasal and sinus passages, and to treat pressure in the middle ear due to eustachian tube blockage.

Mobigesic Tablets — Relieves pain, fever, inflammation, and muscle spasm. Each tablet contains 325 mg of magnesium salicylate and 30 mg of phenyltoloxamine citrate. Ideal for arthritis and injuries of joints and muscles, as well as aches from infections. One of the most useful non-Rx drugs obtainable.

Meclizine Tablets 25 mg — For nausea and vomiting, particularly when due to motion sickness. Dosage is 1 tablet daily. While sold non-Rx only for motion sickness, with prescription this may be taken 3 times daily for dizziness due to inner ear dysfunction. It will work against nausea from virtually any cause.

Benadryl Capsules 25 mg — For antihistamine action these capsules can be taken 1 or 2 every 6 hours. Benadryl is a powerful cough suppressor, the dose being 1 capsule every 6 hours.

Bisacodyl 5 mg — A laxative that works on the large bowel to form a soft stool within 6 to 10 hours. 1 tablet as needed.

Diasorb — The most powerful non-Rx anti-diarrheal agent made, it actually works as well as Imodium, a strong Rx product. Available in liquid or tablets, the latter are easier to carry. Take 4 tablets at the first sign of diarrhea and repeat after each subsequent bowel movement or every 2 hours, whichever comes first. Maximum dose for an adult is 12 tablets per day. Use 2 tablets for children 6-12 and 1 tablet for children 3-6. Tablets should not be chewed, but rather swallowed whole with water. Carry the liquid for children who cannot swallow pills. This product controls diarrhea, but it also does not trap dangerous bacteria or parasites in the bowel as the indiscriminate use of Imodium or Lomotil is apt to due.

Dimacid — High potency antacid tablets. Various brands may be substituted, but do not forget an antacid!

WILDERNESS EXPEDITION MEDICAL KIT
Orthopedic Unit

Quantity	Item
1	Sam Splint
1	Elastic Bandage, 2"
1	Elastic Bandage, 3"
1	Elastic Bandage, 6"
1	Waterproof Tape, 1" x 5 YD
1	Unna Boot, 3" x 10 YDS
2	Webril Orthopedic Padding, 3" x 4 YDS
1	EMT Scissors
1	Over-pak Container for above

Sam Splint — A padded malleable splint that provides enough comfort to be used as a neck collar. It is adequately rigid to splint any extremity and universal so that only one of these need be carried for all splinting needs. This item replaces the necessity for ladder splints, etc. I have never recommended the inclusion of splints in wilderness medical kits, until this product was developed. It weighs less than 5 ounces.

Elastic Bandage, 2 inch
Elastic Bandage. 3 inch
Elastic Bandage, 6 inch
Waterproof Tape, 1" x 5 yds

Obtain good quality bandages that stretch without narrowing and which provide firm, consistent support.

Unna Boot — Casting material. This unusual item is of great assistance in treating sprains of the ankle, but can form supportive bandaging in many areas. It is a gauze strip coated with glycerine, gum arabic, zinc oxide, boric acid, and castor oil. When over-wrapped with an elastic bandage, it forms a durable, almost cast-like, supportive protection that can be easily removed by unwrapping or cutting with scissors. The best size is 3" by 10 yards. The sticky coating easily washes off your hands after wrapping and it serves to protect the skin of the wrapped body part. May be left on for 10 days if necessary.

Webril Orthopedic Padding — 3" x 4 yds. Long strand cotton fiber padding that provides excellent cushioning for splints of all types. I use it frequently to provide a wrap next to the skin, which can then be covered with an elastic (Ace) bandage for a secure, supportive soft cast.

EMT Scissors — Serrated shears that cut through clothing, sheet metal, bandaging, etc.

WILDERNESS EXPEDITION MEDICAL KIT
Field Surgical Unit

Quantity	Item
3	3-0 Nylon Sutures
3	5-0 Nylon Sutures
1	3-0 Gut Suture
1	Needle Holder
1	Curved Hemostats
1	Straight Hemostats
1	Operating Scissors
1	Iris Scissors
1	Bandage Scissors, Lister
1	#3 Stainless Steel Scalpel Handle
3	#11 Scalpel Blades
3	#10 Scalpel Blades
1	Splinter Forceps
1	Adson Tissue Forceps with Teeth
15 pkg	Nu-Gauze, high absorbent, sterile, 2 ply, 3" x 3" pkg/2
1	Bulb Irrigating Syringe
2	Elastomull, Sterile Roller Gauze, 4" x 162"
2	Elastomull, Sterile Roller Gauze, 2 1/2" x 162"
1	Tape, Waterproof 1" x 5 YD
2	Surgical Scrub Brushes, Povidone-Iodine
10 pkg	Q-Tips, Sterile 2/pkg
1	Over-pak Container for above

Suture, Nylon 3-0
Suture, Nylon 5-0
Suture, Plain Gut 3-0

For use in repairing wounds, see pages 92 in the text. Nylon sutures are 18 inches long with a curved needle attached. The plain gut suture is 27 inches long, packed in isopropyl alcohol. All packages are sterile.

Needle Holder — The Mayo-Hegar needle holder, or equal, is necessary to hold the curved suture needle. See text, page 91, for information about its use.

FIGURE 1. MAYO-HEGAR NEEDLE HOLDER

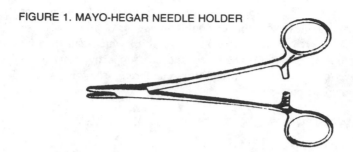

Hemostats, Curved and Straight — These instruments are handy for fine work, such as tagging the ends of suture before tying, suture removal, clamping spurting vessels, and many other gory details. They are useful in disrupting loculations in abscess cavities, as discussed on page 96. Hemostats look much like needle holders, but have shorter handles and are lighter in weight.

Operating Scissors — Sharp pointed scissors designed to cut through macerated tissue, sutures, and other surgical work.

Iris Scissors — Very delicate, for removing small slivers of skin, aiding in removing foreign bodies, cutting tiny sutures, etc. Basically, these are a petite version of operating scissors.

Bandage Scissors, Lister — Bandage scissors have been designed to protect the patient with one blunt end and the other end not only blunt, but with a smooth, snag free knob to allow easy sliding under a tight bandage.

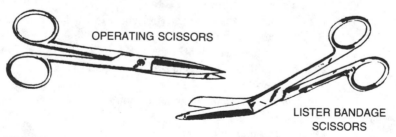

OPERATING SCISSORS

LISTER BANDAGE SCISSORS

SCALPEL, DISPOSABLE, #10 or #11, STERILE

FIGURE 2.

Scalpel Handle, #11 and #10 Blades — Used for a variety of purposes, such as opening an abscess, the blades are sterile and individually sealed in protective packaging. The handle must be sterilized with boiling water, alcohol, etc., before use. The blades are disposable and snap onto the handle. I use a needle holder when snapping them off!

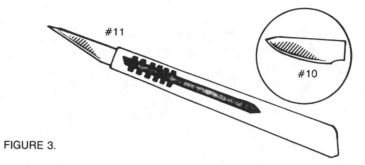

FIGURE 3.

Splinter Forceps — A fine pointed tweezer, for removal of foreign bodies.

Adson Tissue Forceps with Teeth — One side has one tooth, the other two teeth that interlock together for a slip-proof grasp of delicate tissue. Use to hold wound edges together for proper placement of butterfly bandages, tape strips, sutures, or even skin staples.

FIGURE 4. ADSON TISSUE FORCEPS

Bulb Irrigating Syringe — Jets water into a wound with considerable force to remove residue that will promote infection.

WILDERNESS EXPEDITION MEDICAL KIT
Rx Oral/Topical Medication Unit

Quantity	Item
20	Doxycycline 100 mg tablets (antibiotic)
20	Bactrim DS tablets (antibiotic)
24	Tylenol #3 (pain, diarrhea, cough)
24	Atarax 25 mg tablets (nausea, anti-histamine, pain medication augmentation)

1   Topicort .25% Ointment, 1/2 oz tube (skin allergy)
1   Neosporin Ophthalmic Ointment, 1/8 oz tube (eye, ear
       antibiotic)
1   Pontocaine Ophthalmic Ointment .5%, 1/8 oz tube (eye, ear
       anesthetic)
1   Kenalog in Orabase, 5 gm tube (mouth sores)
*   Diamox 250 mg tablets, 10 per person (acute mountain sickness
       prevention)
*   Decadron 4 mg tablets (10 per trip — allergy)(16 per climber at
       high risk — acute mountain sickness)
*   Chloroquine, 300 mg base. Malaria prevention. Taken once
       weekly, beginning 1 week before leaving and continued for 6
       weeks after leaving area with malaria. See text, page 128.

Doxycycline 100 mg — The generic name of an antibiotic that is
useful in treating many travel related diseases. The various sections of
the text dealing with infections will indicate the proper dosage, normally
1 tablet twice daily. Not to be used in children 8 years or younger or
during pregnancy. May cause skin sensitivity on exposure to sunlight,
thus causing an exaggerated sunburn. This does not usually happen,
but be cautious during your first sun exposure when on this product.
Many people traveling in the tropics have used this antibiotic safely.
Very useful in malaria prevention at a dose of 1 tablet daily. Common
brand names are Vibramycin, Vibra-tabs, Vivox, and Doryx.

Bactrim DS — A brand name of a combination of two antibiotics,
namely 800 mg of sulfamethoxazole and 160 mg of trimethoprim.
Another common brand name is Septra DS. Also useful in preventing
or treating traveler's diarrhea and many other infections, its use is
discussed in the appropriate sections of the text. Should not be used at
term of pregnancy or when nursing. Stop using in case of a skin rash
as this may precede a more serious reaction.

Tylenol #3 — The brand name of the combination of 300 mg of
acetaminophen and 30 mg of codeine phosphate, the principle use of
the drug is in the relief of pain. Codeine is one of the most powerful
cough suppression and anti-diarrhea agents known. Also useful in treating abdominal cramping. The dosage of 1 tablet every 4 hours will
normally control a toothache. Maximum dosage is 2 tablets every 3 to
4 hours, augmented with Atarax — see below.

Atarax 25 mg — A brand name of hydroxyzine hydrochloride (note
also the listing under "Vistaril" in the Rx Injectable Medication Unit).
These tablets have multiple uses. They are a very powerful anti-nausea
agent, muscle relaxant, antihistamine, anti-anxiety agent, sleeping pill,

and narcotic potentiator. For sleep 50 mg at bed time; for nausea 25 mg every 4 to 6 hours; to potentiate a narcotic, take a 25 mg tablet with each dose of the pain medication. This medication helps with rashes of all types and has a drying effect on congestion. The injectable version, Vistaril, has identical actions.

Neosporin Ophthalmic Ointment — 1/8 oz tube. Same contents of "triple antibiotic ointment" listed above. Designed for use in the eye — can be melted into the ear. Can be instilled in either location 2 to 3 times daily for infection. Allow to melt.

Pontocaine Ophthalmic Ointment .5% — 1/8 oz tube. Sterile tube for use in eye or ear to numb pain. Do not reapply to eye if pain returns without examining for foreign body very carefully. Apply once daily as needed for eye pain. Do not use in ears if considerable drainage, as an ear drum may have ruptured — avoid use if ear drum is ruptured. Allow to melt.

Kenalog in Orabase — 5 gm tube. For use on mouth sores. May be applied every 3 hours, but generally 3 times daily is sufficient. See discussion, page 40.

Topicort Ointment .25% — This Rx steroid ointment treats severe allergic skin rashes. Ointments work best on dry, scaly lesions. Weeping, blistered areas are best treated with creams, or even wet soaks of dilute salt solution. Dosage is a thin coat twice daily. Occlusive dressings are not required when using this product. Should be used with caution over large body surface areas or in children. Use should be limited to 10 days or less, particularly in the latter cases.

Diamox 250 mg — The brand name of acetazolamide. Used in the prevention of acute mountain sickness for those contemplating rapid ascent to elevations over 9,000 feet. Side effects include tingling of the mouth and fingers, numbness, loss of appetite, and occasional instances of drowsiness and confusion — almost all signs of the acute mountain sickness that one is trying to prevent. Increased urination and rare sun sensitive skin rash is encountered. See text, page 59.

Decdron 4 mg — For allergy 1/2 tablet twice daily after meals for 5 days. For treatment of acute mountain sickness give 4 mg every 6 hours until well below altitude at which symptoms appeared. See text, pages 59 and 104.

Chloroquine 300 mg — Used to prevent malaria. See text, page 128.

WILDERNESS EXPEDITION MEDICAL KIT
Rx Injectable Medication Unit

Quantity	Item
1	Nubain 20 mg/ml, 10 ml multi-use vial (pain)
1	Lidocaine 1% 10 ml multi-use vial (local anesthetic)
12	3 1/2 ml syringes with 25 gauge, 5/8 inch needles
1	Decadron 4 mg/ml, 5 ml multi-use vial (steroid) 1 per trip for allergy; 3 vials per climber at risk for acute mountain sickness
10	Rocephin, 1 gm vials (antibiotic)
1	Sterile water for injection 50 ml multi-use vial (required for mixing Rocephin, 3.6 ml/1 gm vial)
1	Vistaril 50 mg/ml, 10 ml multi-use vial (many uses)
1	Anakit (bee stings — anaphylactic shock, asthma)

Nubain 20mg/ml — strong, synthetic narcotic analgesic, it is available only by prescription, but is not a controlled narcotic with the increased legal problems associated with those substances. Normal adult dose is 10 mg (1/2 ml) given intramuscularly every 3 to 6 hours. Can be mixed with 25 to 50 mg of Vistaril in the same syringe for increased analgesia in severe pain problems. It comes in 10 ml multi-use vials.

Lidocaine 1% — Injection for numbing wounds. Maximum amount to be used in a wound in an adult should be 15 ml. See text, page 94.

Syringes — Many types are available, but for wilderness use I find the 3 1/2 ml with the attached 25 gauge, 5/8 inch needle to be the most universal. The best brand is Monoject as each syringe with needle is packed in a tough, sterile plastic case.

Decadron 4 mg/ml — For use in allergic reactions, give 4 mg daily for 5 days IM. For Acute Mountain Sickness give 4 mg (1 ml) every 6 hours until well below the altitude where symptoms started. See pages 59 and 104.

Rocephin 1 gm vials — A broad spectrum antibiotic of the cephalosporin class, the injectable medication has a wide range of bactericidal activities. Each vial will require 3.6 ml of sterile water to mix the contents. The total mixture per vial would equal 5 ml, which may be given either once daily IM or split into twice daily shots. The 3.5 ml syringe would have to be used twice per vial. The reconstituted medication is stable at room temperatures for 3 days.

Vistaril 50mg/ml — A brand name of hydroxyzine hydrochloride (note also the listing under "Atarax" in the Rx Oral Medication Unit). Uses and dosages are the same as indicated in that listing. Obviously in the treatment of profound vomiting, injection of medication will work better than oral administration. This solution can be mixed in the same syringe as the Nubain for administration as 1 injection.

Anakit — A commercial kit consisting of a multiple use syringe of epinephrine (Adrenalin) and chewable antihistamine tablets, with alcohol wipes and bandage. One half the syringe amount (.3 ml) can be given before a twist is required to administer the second half of the injection. .3 ml is the standard adult dose required to treat anaphylactic shock due to severe allergic reactions from bee stings, etc. See page 113.

INCIDENTAL ITEMS USED BY THE TEAM MEDIC — Occasional use of items brought along for various other purposes is made for medical reasons. From the cook the medic needs to borrow baking soda, salt and sugar in the management of profound diarrhea. Soap for cleaning wounds may also be obtained from the kitchen, if a surgical scrub is not carried in the medical kit. Granulated sugar sprinkled on abrasions is a field expedient method of preventing infection, when there are no antibiotics available.

Each fishing kit should have wire cutters, possibly required to remove a hook from people, as well as fish. It may also be used to destroy a zipper if someone has caught their skin. Wool clothing is needed to prevent and treat hypothermic conditions, especially wool hat, wool socks and wool shirts. Having adequate sleeping bags, and choosing those that twin, may prove life-saving in hypothermic conditions. A full treatment of modern synthetic fabrics is provided in my book *Hypothermia*, listed in Appendix B.

Matches are frequently a life-saver and should be available on each trip. And perhaps the entire party would benefit with a daily vitamin supplement, such as the formulation in the popular Miles Laboratories *One-A-Day with Iron*.

FEVER — CHILLS — The average oral temperature of a resting individual is 98.6°F, and in active individuals 99.0°F. Rectal temperatures are 0.5 to 1°F higher. Temperature rise in a human will result in the heart rate increasing 10 beats per minute faster than the patient's normal resting temperature. This is a useful field method of judging temperature, if each individual knows what his resting pulse is. Some diseases cause a peculiar drop in heart rate even in the face of an obviously high temperature. The most notable of these is typhoid fever, page 122 and yellow fever, page 129.

Although injury and exposure can cause elevated body temperature, fever is usually the result of infection. The cause of the fever should be sought and treated. If pain or infection is located in the ear, throat, etc., refer to the appropriate anatomical area listed in the Instant Reference Clinical Index.

If other symptoms beside fever are present (diarrhea, cough, etc.), see the cross references listing these symptoms in the Instant Reference Clinical Index in order to provide treatment to alleviate the suffering of these maladies. This may diagnose the underlying disease which would have a specific treatment indicated in the text.

The wilderness approach to therapy may be quite different from that used in clinical medicine. In the wilderness when in doubt about whether or not the fever is due to viral, bacterial, or other infectious causes — treat with antibiotic from your Rx medical kit. Initially, give the patient doxycycline 100 mg, 1 tablet every 12 hours and continue until the fever has broken and then reduce the dosage to 1 tablet daily for an additional 4 days. this will conserve medication while providing adequate antibiotic coverage to a suspected bacterial infection. If it is possible that the patient has a strep throat (see page 37), continue coverage for a total of 10 days. If you are not carrying the Rx kit, then treat the symptoms using the medications described in your nonRx kits. In either case, rest is important until the patient is again free of fever and has a sense of well being.

Chills are a state of shivering with a sense of coldness — not related to hypothermia as discussed on page 62. Chills are usually followed by fever. They frequently indicate the onset of a bacterial infection which should be treated with an antibiotic as described above.

LETHARGY — Lethargy, or prolonged tiredness or malaise, is a non-localizing symptom such as fever or muscle ache (myalgia). Pain, however, *is* a localizing symptom that points to the organ system which may be the cause of such things as lethargy, fever, or a generally ill feeling. Frequently after a brief period of a few days of lethargy — or at times even hours — localizing symptoms develop and the cause of the lethargy can be determined to be an infection of the throat, ear, etc.

At times a chronic condition is the source of the lethargy, such as anemia, leukemia, low thyroid function, depression, occult or low grade infection, mental depression, or even physical exhaustion. The latter we would expect to be obvious from the history of the preceding level of activity and strength should return within a few days.

Anemia can present due to chronic blood loss from cancer, ulcers, menstrual problems, lack of adequate formation due to low iron, leukemia and other cancers in the bone marrow, etc. A chronic anemia can be identified by looking at the color of the skin inside the lower eye lids. Pull the lower lid down and look at it. Compare to another person. Normally the thin skin is very orange colored, even if the cheeks are pale. If the color is a blanched, white — then anemia is very likely. Another good indication of anemia is an increase in the pulse rate of more than 30 beats per minute in the standing position compared to the prone (or laying down) position.

If other symptoms are present such as nausea, one must think of hepatitis (see page 75), or if preceded by a severe sore throat then infectious mononcleosis (see page 37). Lethargy is one of the most common presenting complaints which I see in my office. The full length of possible diagnosis is lengthy and requires careful evaluation and frequently laboratory tests. If the problem is not depression, then regardless of the cause, the person needs rest, proper nutrition, and adequate shelter.

PAIN — Adequate pain management can be a mixture of proper medication and attitude — the attitude of both the victim and the medic being important. A calm, professional approach to problems will lessen anxiety, panic, and pain. Pain is an important symptom that tells you something is wrong. It generally "localizes" or points to the exact cause of the trouble, so that pain in various parts of the body will be your clue that a problem exists and that specific treatment may be required to eliminate it. Refer to the *Instant Clinical Reference Index* for areas of the body (such as ear, abdomen, etc.) where pain exists to read further about diagnosis and for further specific treatments of the causes of pain.

From the Non-Rx Oral Medication Unit provide the victim with Mobigesic, 1 or 2 tablets every 4 hours. Mobigesic is probably the best pain medication that can be obtained without a prescription, providing anti-inflammatory, pain, and muscle relaxant actions. It is fully described on page 7. It is particularly good for orthopedic injuries or whenever muscle sprains and contusions are encountered. It is also ideal for menstrual cramps, tension headache, and it is relatively safe to use in head injuries. It can also be used for the muscle aches and fever from viral and bacterial infections. Its anti- inflammatory abilities make it ideal for treatment of tendonitis, bursitis, or arthritic pain. If you do not have Mobigesic available, obtain 200 mg tablets of ibuprofen which is now available without prescription as the best alternate drug. Brand names generally available are Nuprin, Medipren, and Advil. Lacking this, obtain aspirin (ASA) or Tylenol (acetaminophen) for your non-prescription kit.

FOR SEVERE PAIN you may have to rely on the Rx Oral Medication Unit component Tylenol #3, taking 1 tablet every 4 hours. One of these tablets is generally enough to eliminate a bad toothache. For serious injury, 2 tablets at a time provide fairly substantial pain relief. They can be augmented by also giving the victim 1 or 2 Atarax 25 mg tablets every 4 to 6 hours. This medication helps eliminate the nausea associated with high codeine dosages and from my experience it also potentiates the Tylenol #3 so that it works more effectively.

If you are carrying the Rx Injectable Medication Unit, severe pain can be treated with an injection of 10 mg of Nubain (½ ml of the strength listed in the kit). This can be potentiated with Vistaril 25 mg or 50 mg injection. Vistaril and Nubain can be mixed in the same syringe. They both sting upon injection.

ITCH — As itch is a sensation that is transmitted by pain fibers, all pain medications can be used in alleviating itch sensations. Itch is also an indication of something being awry and possibly requiring specific treatment. The most common causes are local allergic reactions, such as poisonous plants (page 104); fungal infections (page 104); and insect bites or infestations (pages 118 to 120 or look under specific causes in the index).

General principles of treatment include further avoidance of the offending substance (not so easy in the case of mosquitos). Avoid applying heat to an itchy area, as this flares it worse. Avoid scratching or rubbing, this also increases the reaction. If weeping blisters have formed, apply wet soaks with a clean cloth or gauze. While plain water soaks will help, making a solution of boric acid, epsom salts, or even regular table salt will help dry the lesions and alleviate some of the itch. Make an approximately 10% solution weight to volume of water.

Cream based preparations work on moist lesions, while ointments are more effective on dry, scaly ones. The Non-Rx Topical/Bandaging Unit contains .5% hydrocortisone cream which, while safe to use, is generally not very effective against severe allergic dermatitis. To potentiate it, one should apply it four times daily and then cover the area with an occlusive dressing, such as cellophane or a piece of polybag. The Rx Oral/Topical Medication Unit contains Topicort .25% cream which is strong enough to adequately treat allergic dermatitis with light coats applied twice daily. Athlete's foot and skin rashes in the groin or in skin folds are generally fungal and should not be treated with these creams. They may seem to provide temporary relief, but they can actually worsen fungal infections. For possible fungal infections, apply the Miconazole Cream 2% twice daily from the Non-Rx Topical/Bandaging Unit.

Oral medications are frequently required to treat severe skin reactions and itch. The Non-Rx Oral Medication Unit contains Benadryl 25 mg. Taken 1 or 2 capsules every 6 hours, it is one of the most effective anti-histamines made. The Rx Oral Medication Unit contains Atarax 25 mg. It is very effective in treating the symptom of itch and in its anti-histamine actions. Take 1 or 2 tablets every 6 hours. These medications are safe to use on all sorts of itch problems. If one is suffering from an asthma attack they should not be used, however, as they tend to dry out the lung secretions and make the illness worse.

Hives are the result of a severe allergic reaction. Commonly called welts, these raised red blotches appear rapidly, have a red border around a clearer skin area in the center, something that is referred to as an "annular" lesion. As these can and do appear over large surfaces of the skin, treatment with a cream is of little help. Use the Benadryl or Atarax as indicated above. In case of a concurrent asthmatic condition or the development of shock, treat as indicated under "anaphylactic shock" on page 113.

SHOCK— THIS IS A LIFE THREATENING EMERGENCY and must be treated promptly. Insure that an adequate airway is established. (Note further discussion under RESCUE BREATHING, page 49). Assess cardiac status — place hand over a carotid artery, located in the upper neck along side of the trachea (windpipe). In shock the patient will have a weak, rapid pulse — in adults the rate will be over 140, children over 180 beats per minute. If there is doubt about a pulse being present, listen to the bare chest — if cardiac standstill is present, institute cardio-pulmonary resusitation (see discussion under CARDIAC COMPRESSION, page 50). Elevate the legs to 45° to obtain a rapid return of venous blood to the heart — however, if there has been a head injury, lay the patient flat. If external bleeding is evident, stop with direct pressure (use a bare hand, if necessary, until an adequate bandage can be obtained or fashioned). Attempt to treat the underlying cause of the shock — a quick history may well elicit the cause of the shock and appropriate treatment can be devised from the field expedient methods listed in this book.

An important aspect of the correction of shock is to identify and treat the underlying cause. Shock can be caused by burns, electrocution, hypothermia, bites, stings, bleeding, fractures, pain, hyperthermia, high altitude cerebral edema, profound diarrhea, illness, rough handling, just to name a few. Obviously, at times the history of the patient's past 24 hours is helpful in making the correct diagnosis — most frequently a quick glance is enough to tell the tale. Each of these underlying causes is discussed separately in the text.

EYE PROBLEMS — Pain and irritation of the eye can be devastating. Causes are listed in the table below:

TABLE 1
Symptoms and Signs of Eye Pathology

	Vision Loss	Pain	Red	Drainage	Tissue Swelling
Trauma	x	xx	xx	x	x
Foreign Body		xx	xx	xx	
Infection-bacteria		x	xx	xx	x
-viral		x	xx	x	x
-sty		x	xx		xx
Allergy		xx		x	x
Corneal Ulcers	x	xx			
Snow Blindness	x	xx	xx	x	
Strain		x			
Glaucoma	x	xx			
Spontaneous Subconjunctival Hemorrhage			xx		

xx   A frequent or intense symptom
x   Common, less intense symptom
Blank   Less likely to produce this symptom

Eye Patch and Bandaging Techniques — In case of evidence of infection, do not use an eye patch or splint, but have the patient wear dark glasses, a wide brimmed hat, or take other measures to decrease light exposure. Wash the eye with clean water by dabbing with wet, clean cloth, every two hours to remove pus and excess secretions. Apply antibiotics as indicated under eye infections.

Eye patch techniques must allow for gentle closure of the eyelid and retard blinking activity. Generally both eyes must be patched for this to succeed. Simple strips of tape taping the eyelids shut may suffice. In case of trauma, an annular ring of cloth may be constructed to pad the eye without pressure over the eyeball. A simple eye patch with over-size gauze or cloth may work fine, as the bone of the orbital rim around the eye acts to protect the eyeball which is recessed.

Serious injury requires patching both eyes, as movement in the injured eye will decrease if movement in the unaffected eye is also controlled. It generally helps to have the victim kept in a 30 degree head elevated position and at rest after eye injury. A severe blow to one eye may cause temporary blindness in both eyes which can resolve in hours to days. Obviously, a person with loss of vision should be treated by a physician if possible. Eye dressings must be removed, or at least changed in 24 hours.

If the victim has suffered a corneal abrasion or after removing foreign bodies, the best splint is the tension patch. Start by placing two gauze pads over the shut eye, requesting the patient to keep his eyes closed until the bandaging is completed. The patient may help hold the gauze in place. Three pieces of one inch wide tape are ideal, long enough to extend from the center of the forehead to just below the cheek bone. Fasten the first piece of tape to the center of the forehead, extending the tape diagonally downward across the eye patch. The second and third strips are applied parallel to the first strip, one above and the other below. This dressing will result in firm splinting of the bandaged eye.

Foreign Body — The most common problems in the wilderness will be foreign body, abrasion, and infection (conjunctivitis). Therapy for these problems is virtually the same, except that it is very important to remove any foreign body that may be present.

The initial step in examining the painful eye is to remove the pain. One of the lessons drilled into medical students is to never, never write a prescription for eye anesthesia agents (such as the Pontocaine .5% which I recommend for the Rx kit). The reason is the patient may use it, obtain relief, and then not have the eye carefully examined for a foreign body. Eventually, this foreign body may cause an ulcer to form in the cornea doing profound damage. When using the Pontocaine, remember that it is very important to find and remove any foreign body. Pull down on the lower lid and instill a thin ribbon of the Pontocaine ophthalmic ointment. Have the patient close their eye and let them rest with it shut, thus giving time for the medication to melt and anesthetize the eye. This medication burns when initially instilled in the eye. This will increase the level of pain for a brief period until the medication takes effect.

After the patient has calmed down, have them open the eye and look straight ahead. Very carefully shine a pen light at the cornea from one side to see if a minute speck becomes visible. By moving the light back and forth, one might see movement of a shadow on the iris of the eye and thus confirm the presence of a foreign body. The Pontocaine ointment will give a gooey appearance to the cornea that may mimic a foreign body. Have the victim blink to move any medication around. A point that consistently stays put with blinking is probably a foreign body.

In making the foreign body examination, also be sure to check under the eyelids. Evert the upper lid over a Q-tip stick, thus examining not only the eyeball, but also the under-surface of the eyelid. This surface may be gently brushed with the cotton applicator to eliminate minute particles. Always use a fresh Q-tip when touching the eye or eyelid each additional time.

Foreign body removal may first be attempted by flushing the eye with clean water. The bulb syringe is ideal for this maneuver. Blinking the submersed eye may also suffice.

When a foreign body has been identified stuck on the cornea, take a sterile, or at least a clean, Q-tip and approach the foreign body from the side. Gently prod it with the Q-tip handle until it is loosened. The surface of the eye will indent under the pressure of this scraping action. Indeed the surface of the cornea will be scratched in the maneuver, but it will quickly heal. Once the foreign body has been dislodged, if it does not stick to the wooden handle, but slides loose along the cornea surface, use the cotton portion to touch it for removal.

A stoic individual, particularly one accustomed to contact lenses, might be able to undergo a non-complicated foreign body removal without the use of Pontocaine, but using anesthesia makes the patient more comfortable and cuts down on the blink reflex (interference).

Foreign bodies stuck in the cornea can be very stubborn and resist removal. At times it is necessary to pick them loose with the sharp point of a #11 scalpel blade or the tip of a needle (I frequently use an 18 gauge needle). Anesthesia with Pontocaine will be a necessity for this procedure. Scraping with these instruments will cause a more significant scrape to the cornea surface, but under these circumstances it may have to be accepted. I would leave stubborn foreign bodies for removal by a physician in all but the most desperate circumstances. If you have a difficult time removing an obvious foreign body from the surface of the cornea, a wait of two to three days may allow the cornea to ulcerate slightly so that removal with the Q-tip stick may be *much* easier. Deeply lodged foreign bodies will have to be left for surgical removal.

A painless foreign body may not be a foreign body. It could be a rust ring left behind after a bit of ferrous, or iron containing, material has fallen out of the eye after having been lodged for a short time. They should be ignored in the wilderness setting.

The history of striking objects may indicate a deeper penetration than one would expect from blowing debris. A puncture wound of the eyelid mandates careful examination of the cornea surface for evidence of a penetrating foreign body. These injuries must be seen by a physician for surgical care. Evacuation is necessary. If this is impossible, the eye must be patched, examined for infection twice daily, and treated with antibiotic both by mouth and with ointment.

After removal of a foreign body, or even after scraping the eye while attempting to remove one, instill some antibiotic. The prescription kit should contain Neosporin Ophthalmic in a 1/8 oz tube. This is instilled by pulling down on the lower lid and laying a ribbon along the everted margin. Have the patient close the eye to allow the medication to melt. In the same manner apply a small amount of the Pontocaine Ophthalmic to provide pain relief. Pontocaine should not be used more than 4 times a day and for no longer than two days. Continued use may hinder the natural healing process and may cover a significant injury or mask the presence of an additional foreign body. Tylenol #3, 1 tablet every four to six hours may be given for pain.

About the best non-prescription eye antiseptic for this purpose would be yellow oxide of mercury 2% ophthalmic ointment, also in 1/8 oz tubes and used as above. Neosporin and Polysporin ointment in large tubes manufactured by Burroughs-Welcome is safe to use in the eye and is not a prescription product. However, the manufacturer cannot recommend the use of these large tubes for this purpose. Mobigesic, 2 tablets every four to six hours may be provided for pain.

Eye Abrasion — Abrasions may be caused by a glancing blow from a wood chip, a swinging branch, even from blowing dirt, embers, ice or snow. The involved eye should be anesthetized with Rx Pontocaine and protected with the Rx Neosporin ophthalmic ointment or the non-Rx yellow oxide of mercury 2%. Make sure that a foreign body has not been over-looked.

In cold wind be sure to protect your eyes from the effects of both blowing particles of ice and the wind itself. Grey Owl, in his interesting book, *Tales of an Empty Cabin*, tells how he was walking on one of his long trips through the backwoods along a windswept frozen lake when suddenly he lost sight of the tree line. He felt that he must be in a white-out, so he turned perpendicular to the wind and hiked toward the shore. Suddenly he bumped into a tree and then realized that he was blind! He saved himself only by digging a snow cave and staying put for three days. He wondered how many good woodsmen were lost on their trap lines by such a similar incident, apparently a temporary opacification of the cornea from the cold wind.

Snow Blindness — This severely painful condition is primarily caused by ultraviolet B rays of the sun which are considerably reflected by snow (85%), water (10-100%), and sand (17%). Thin cloud layers allow the transmission of this wavelength, while filtering out infra-red (heat) rays of the sun. Thus, it is possible on a rather cool, overcast day under bright snow conditions to become sunburned or snow blind.

Properly approved (ANSI) sunglasses will block 99.8% of the ultraviolet B wavelength. Suitable glasses should be tagged as meeting these standards[1]. Non-prescription glasses must be proper fitting and ideally provide side protection. A suitable retention strap must be worn, as I recently once again learned while rafting on the Green River in Colorado. And for those of us who must learn these things more than once, a second pair of glasses — particularly if prescription lenses are worn — is essential. Lacking sunglasses, any field expedient method of eliminating glare, such as slit glasses made from wood or any material at hand, to include the ubiquitous bandana, will help. An important aspect of snow blindness is the delayed onset of symptoms. The pain and loss of vision may not be evident until after damaging exposure has been sustained.

Snow blindness is a self limiting affliction. However, not only is the actual loss of vision a problem, but so is the terrible pain, usually described as feeling like red hot pokers were massaging the eye sockets. Lacking any first aid supplies the treatment would be gentle eye patch and the application of cold packs as needed for pain relief. Generally both eyes are equally affected with a virtual total loss of vision. If there is partial sight and the party is moving, then patching the most affected eye may be practical. Otherwise, rest both eyes.

The prescription Pontocaine ophthalmic ointment will help ease the pain, but long term use can delay eye surface healing. Oral pain medication will be of help and should be used. The severe pain can last from hours to several days. In case a drainage of pus, or crusting of the eye-lids occurs, start antibiotic ophthalmic ointment applications as indicated in the section on conjunctivitis.

Conjunctivitis, or Infections of the Eye Surface — An infection of the eye will be heralded by a scratchy feeling, almost indistinguishable from a foreign body in the eye. The sclera or white of the eye will be reddened. Generally the eye will be matted shut in the morning with pus or granular matter.

Infections are generally caused by bacteria, but viral infections also occur. Viral infections tend to have a blotchy red appearance over the white of the eye, while bacterial infections have a generalized red appearance. The drainage in bacterial infections tends to be pus, while virus usually cause a watery discharge.

[1]The American National Standards Institute, or ANSI, establishes specifications for many manufactured products.

Allergic conjunctivitis will result in faint pink eyes and a clear drainage. There are frequently other symptoms of allergy such as runny nose, no fever, and no lymph node enlargement. With either viral or bacterial conjunctivitis, look for fever and possibly lymph node enlargement in the neck. Runny nose and sinus infection are frequently present also.

Be sure that a foreign body is not the cause of the reddish eye and infection. If so, it must be removed.

Rinse with clean water frequently during the day. Eye infections such as common bacterial conjunctivitis, the most common infection, are self limiting and will generally clear themselves within two weeks. They can become much worse, however, so medical attention should be sought. Do not patch, but protect the eyes from sunlight. When one eye is infected, treat both eyes as the infection spreads easily to the non-infected eye.

Treatment from the non-Rx supplies would consist of using yellow oxide of mercury 2% 3 times a day for 5 to 7 days. From the Rx supplies one could use the Neosporin ophthalmic ointment 3 times a day for 5 to 7 days. Steroids should not be placed in the eye if there is any chance that a viral infection may be present, as this could cause severe corneal damage when the virus is a herpes simplex. If the infection fails to show improvement within 48 hours, probably the antibiotic will not be effective, or there may be a missed foreign body present, or the patient may be allergic to the antibiotic or something else such as pollen in the environment. Switch medications in the case of no improvement after 48 hours. When no other antibiotic ointment is available, use oral antibiotic such as Bactrim DS, one tablet twice daily, or doxycycline 100 mg, one capsule twice daily. If the eye is improving, continue use as indicated above.

Iritis is an inflammatory disease of the eye having the general appearance of conjunctivitis, but while in the latter the reddish color fades to white near the iris of the eye (the colored part), with iritis the rim of sclera (white of the eye) around the iris is more inflamed or reddened than the white portion further out. Provide sun protection. Give aspirin or other pain medication if available. Have patient see a physician immediately. The non-Rx treatment will consist of giving the patient Mobigesic 2 tablets every 3 hours. Instill yellow oxide of mercury ophthalmic 2% three times a day. Provide sun protection. The prescription treatment would be Tylenol #3, 1 or 2 tablets every 3 to 4 hours. Instill Neosporin ophthalmic ointment three times a day. Provide sun protection. This patient would benefit from eye dilation and possibly local steroid use under a physician's care.

As iritis progresses, the red blush near the iris will become more pronounced and spasm of muscle used in operation of the iris will cause the pupil to become irregular. With further progression it is possible for the pupil (anterior chamber) to become cloudy, for cataracts and glaucoma to develop, and serious scarring of eye tissues to develop. Sometimes a profound conjunctivitis or corneal abrasion will cause an iritis that will clear as the problem clears. Some cases of mild iritis can be cleared with agents that dilate the pupil without steroid use. All cases of iritis require treatment by an ophthalmologist.

Contact Lenses — The increased popularity of contact lens wear means that several problems associated with their use have also increased. The lenses are of two basic types. The hard, or rigid, lens which generally is smaller and does not extend beyond the iris, and the soft lens which does extend beyond the iris onto the white of the eye. Soft lenses have been designed for extended wear. Hard lens use requires frequent removal, as the delicate cornea of the eye obtains oxygen from the environment and nutrient from eye secretions. These lenses interfere with this process and therefore are detrimental to the cornea. Examine the eyes of all unconscious persons for the existence of hard lenses and remove them if found. It is probably best to remove soft lenses also as some are not designed for extended use and may also damage the eye.

The patient may have pain from the migration of the lens into one of the recesses of the conjunctiva, or possibly only have noted a loss of refractive correction. At times the complaint is a sudden "I have lost my contact lens!" Never forget to look in the eye as the possible hiding spot for the lens. Examine the eye as described in the section on foreign bodies in the eye. When dealing with a hard lens, use topical anesthesia as described if necessary and available. If the lens is loose, slide it over the pupil and allow the patient to remove it as they usually do. If the lens is adherent, rinse with eye irrigation solution or clean water and try again. If a corneal abrasion exists, patch as indicated above after the lens is removed.

The soft lens may generally be squeezed between the fingers and literally "popped" off. A special rubber pincer is sold that can aid in this maneuver. Hard lenses may also be removed with a special rubber suction cup device.

If the patient is unconscious, the hard lens will have to be removed. Lacking the suction cup device there are two different maneuvers which may be employed. One is the vertical technique. In this method, move the lens to the center of the eye over the pupil. Then press down on the lower lid, over the lower edge of the contact lens. Next squeeze the eyelids together, thus popping the lens out between them as indicated in figure 5.

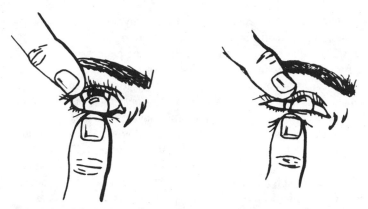

FIGURE 5. CONTACT LENS REMOVAL — VERTICAL TECHNIQUE

In the lateral technique, the lens is slid to the outside corner of the eye. By tugging on the facial skin near the eye in a downward and outward direction, the lens can pop over the skin edge and be easily removed. See figure 6.

FIGURE 6. CONTACT LENS REMOVAL — HORIZONTAL TECHNIQUE

The unconscious patient should have antibiotic salve placed in their eyes and the lids taped or patched shut to prevent drying. These patches should be removed when needed for neurological checks, and certainly upon regaining consciousness.

If removal of the lens must be prolonged, safe storage will have to be provided. With regard to hard lenses, the ideal would be marked containers that padded the lens in such a way that they would not buffet around or otherwise become scratched. Small vials, labelled R and L, filled with a fluff of clean material, taped together and placed in a safe location, would be ideal.

Soft contact lenses must be protected from dehydration. It is always proper to store them in normal saline. This solution can be prepared by adding 1 1/2 oz table salt to 1 pint of water. If the patient has a special solution for their lenses in their possession, of course use it.

Leaving most hard contact lenses in the eyes longer than 12 hours can result in corneal ulceration. While not serious, this can be a very painful experience. At times even an iritis may result. This condition almost always resolves on its own within one day. The history is the major clue that the diagnosis is correct. If the condition failed to clear within 24 hours, other problems should be looked into such as corneal laceration, foreign body, or eye infection. After removal of the contact lens, place cool cloths on the eyes or ice packs to the eyes. This patient should be evaluated by a physician to confirm the diagnosis. Provide protection from sunlight. Patching both eyes while at rest will be of help. Give aspirin or other pain medication if available.

Sties and Chalazia — These infections of the eyelid can cause scratching of the cornea surface. Often the victim thinks that something is in the eye when, in fact, one of these small pimples is forming. The sty is an infection along a hair follicle on the eyelid margin. The chalazion is an infection of an oil gland on the inner lid margin. The patient will have redness, pain, and swelling along the edge of the upper or lower eye lid. At times the eye will be red with evidence of infection, or conjunctivitis. An eyelid may be swollen and without the pimple formation when this problem first develops. There should not be extensive swelling around the eye. That could represent a *periorbital cellulitis* which is a serious infection requiring treatment with injectable antibiotics.

Make sure that a foreign body is not causing the symptoms. Check the eye and eye lids as indicated in that section. While so checking, ascertain if there is a pimple formation that confirms the diagnosis. If it is on the upper lid and it is scratching the eye while blinking, patch the eye and send to a physician for treatment. If no medical care is available, have the patient place warm compresses on the eye for 20 minutes every two hours to cause the sty to come to a head. When it does, it may spontaneously break and drain. If it does not in two days, open it with a flick of a #11 scalpel blade or needle. Continue the warm compresses and provide medication as below. Patch as indicated above. If only non-Rx medication is available, instill the 2% yellow oxide of mercury 3 times daily. If Rx supplies are available, then instill Neosporin ophthalmic ointment three times a day (note discussion concerning the use of OTC antibiotic ointment in the eye on page 23, however). If the lid is quite swollen, give the patient Bactrim DS by mouth twice daily or doxycycline 100 mg twice daily. Once localized and draining, the oral antibiotic will not be necessary.

Spontaneous Subconjunctival Hemorrhage — This condition presents as bright bleeding over a portion of the white, or conjunctiva, of the eye. It spreads out over a period of 12 to 48 hours, then re-absorbs slowly over the next 7 to 21 days, first turning the conjunctiva yellowish as the blood is degenerated. There should not be any pain with this, although some people may report a vague "full" feeling in the eye. It normally occurs without cause, but can appear after blunt trauma, or violent coughing, sneezing, or vomiting. No treatment is necessary.

Blunt Trauma to the Eye — The immediate treatment is to immobilize the injured eye as soon as possible by patching both eyes and moving the patient only by litter. Double vision could mean that there has been a fracture of the orbit of the eye or that there is a lesion within the central nervous system. Double vision is sometimes caused by swelling of tissue behind the eyelid. A hyphema may appear, which is a collection of blood in the anterior chamber of the eye. The blood settles in front of the pupil, behind the cornea.

Patch as indicated in the section on serious injury eye patch techniques. Patients with hyphema and serious blunt trauma should be evacuated to a physician for care. Have the patient sit with head up, from 45 to 90 degrees to allow blood to pool at the lower edge of the anterior chamber. Check the eye twice daily for drainage which might indicate infection. If infection develops, treat with oral antibiotics such as Bactrim DS twice daily or doxycycline 100 mg twice daily. Neosporin ointment may be instilled three times daily if a conjunctivitis ensues. Treat with oral pain medications such as Tylenol #3, 1 or 2 tablets every 4 hours. Give Atarax 25 mg 4 times daily as needed to potentiate the pain medication and help alleviate nausea or 50 mg 4 times daily if required to calm the patient.

Provide the strongest pain medications required to prevent the injured patient from grimacing and squeezing the injured eye, thus possibly compromising the eye contents even more. Small corneal or scleral lacerations may require no treatment at all, but these should be seen and evaluated by a physician if at all possible. It should be noted that severe injury to one eye may even cause blindness to develop in the other eye due to "sympathetic ophthalmia," which is probably an allergic response to eye pigment of the injured eye entering the victim's blood stream.

Allergic Conjunctivitis — The common wilderness causes are sensitivity to inhaled pollens and irritation with wood smoke. This problem is usually associated with a runny nose (rhinitis) and at times swelling of the eyelids. Rarely there will be a generalized skin itching and the appearance of welts (urticaria). In severe cases there can be considerable swelling of the conjunctival covering of the white of the eye (sclera), forming what appears as fluid-filled sacs over the sclera of the eye (but not covering the cornea). This puffy tissue generally has a light pink tinge to it.

From the non-Rx supplies give Actifed 1 tablet 4 times a day and use the tetrahydrozoline eye drops, 2 in each eye every 3 or 4 hours as needed.

Glaucoma — Glaucoma is the rise of pressure within the eyeball. The most common form (open angle glaucoma) generally is not encountered before the age of 40. The patient notes halos around lights, mild headaches, loss of vision to the sides (peripheral field cuts), and loss of ability to see well at night. The external eye usually appears normal. This frequently affects both eyes. This condition is generally of gradual onset so that the patient can consult a physician upon returning from the bush.

Initial treatment is with a prescription drug, one drop of 0.5% pilocarpine. It would not be necessary to carry this particular medication, except to treat this condition. This problem should be detected by the pre-trip physical examination. Everyone over the age of 40 should have their intra-ocular pressure tested prior to departure.

Acute glaucoma (narrow angle glaucoma) is much less common than open angle glaucoma, but is much more spectacular in onset. Acute glaucoma is characterized by a rapid rise in pressure of the fluid within the eyeball causing blurred vision, severe pain in the eye, and even abdominal distress from vagal nerve stimulation. An acute attack can sometimes be broken with pilocarpine, but often needs emergency surgery. A thorough eye examination should be done before the trip to discover those eyes with narrow angles that could result in acute glaucoma. In eyes likely to develop acute glaucoma, a laser iridectomy can be done as an outpatient to prevent an acute narrow angle glaucoma attack.

NASAL CONGESTION is caused by an allergic reaction to pollen, dust, or other allergens, and viral or bacterial upper respiratory infections. Bacterial infections will require an antibiotic to cure, but otherwise all are treated similarly for symptomatic relief. Use Actifed, which should be taken 1 tablet every 6 hours as needed for nasal congestion. Treat for discomfort with the Mobigesic from the non-Rx supplies or

Tylenol #3 from the Rx Oral/Topical Unit as needed. Drink lots of liquid to prevent the mucous from becoming too thick. If the patient has no fever, do not give an antibiotic. A low grade temperature is probably viral and still does not warrant an antibiotic. If a temperature greater than 101 F is present, then treat with antibiotic such as the doxycycline 100 mg twice daily from the Rx supplies.

FOREIGN BODY IN NOSE — Foul drainage from one nostril is very suspicious of a foreign body. In adults the history of something being placed up the nose would of course help in the diagnosis. In a child drainage from one nostril must be considered to be a foreign body until ruled out. Have the patient try to blow his nose to remove the foreign body. With an infant it may be possible for a parent to gently puff into the baby's mouth to force the object out of the nose. While having a nasal speculum would be ideal, using the emergency kit one can improvise by using the mosquito or Hartman hemostats. Spread the tips apart after placing them just inside the nostril. One can stretch the nostril without pain quite extensively. Shine a light into the nostril passage and attempt to spot the foreign body. Try to grasp the object with another forcep or other instrument under direct visualization in this manner. If the foreign material is actually debris, say a capsule that broke in the patient's mouth and which was sneezed into the nostrils, it is best to irrigate this material out rather than attempting to cleanse with a Q-tip, etc. Place a bulb or irrigation syringe in the clear nostril. With the patient repeating an "eng" sound, flush water and hopefully the debris out the opposite nostril.

After removing a foreign body, be sure to check the nostril again for an additional one. Try not to push a foreign body down the back of the patient's throat where they may choke on it. If this is unavoidable, have the patient face down and bend over to decrease the chance of choking.

NOSE BLEED (Epistaxis) — If nose bleeding is caused from a contusion to the nose, the bleeding is usually self limited. Bleeding that starts without trauma is generally more difficult to stop. Most bleeding is from small arteries located near the front of the nose partition, or nasal septum. The best treatment is direct pressure. Have the victim squeeze the nose between his fingers for ten minutes by the clock (a very long time when there is no clock to watch). If this fails, squeeze another ten minutes. Do not blow the nose for this will dislodge clots and start the bleeding all over again. If the bleeding is severe, have the victim sit up to prevent choking on blood and to aid in the reduction of the blood pressure in the nose. Cold compresses do little good.

Continued bleeding can result in shock. This will in turn decrease the bleeding. The sitting position is mandatory to prevent choking on blood from a severe bleed and, as indicated above, will aid in the reduction of blood pressure in the nose.

Another technique that can be tried is to wet a gauze strip thoroughly with the epinephrine from the syringe in the Anakit, a component of the prescription medical kit. Those having only non-prescription medical supplies will have to use the tetrahydrozoline eye drops, which will not be as powerful in their action. First clear the nose of blood clot so the gauze can be in direct contact with the nasal membranes. Have the victim blow their nose or use the irrigation syringe. Place the epinephrine soaked gauze in the nose and apply pinching pressure. The epinephrine can act as a vaso-constrictor to decrease the blood flow and allow clotting. Pinch for ten minute increments. The gauze may removed after the bleeding has stopped.

NOSE FRACTURE — A direct blow causing a nasal fracture is associated with pain, swelling, and nasal bleeding. The pain is usually point tender, so that very light touch will result in an exact place along the spine of the nose where the pain is intense. While the bleeding from trauma to the nose can initially be intense, it seldom lasts more than a few minutes. Apply cold compress, if available. Allow the patient to pinch their nose to aid in reducing bleeding, if necessary.

If the nose is laterally displaced (shoved to one side), push it back into place. More of these fractures have been treated by coaches on the playing field than have been reduced by doctors. If it is a depressed fracture, a specialist will have to properly elevate the fragments. As soon as the person returns from the bush have him seen by a physician, but this is not a reason for expensive medical evacuation. Provide pain medication, but this should only be necessary for a few doses. It is rare to need to pack a bleeding nose due to trauma and it should be avoided if possible due to the increased pain it would cause.

EAR RELATED PROBLEMS — Problems with the ear involve pain, loss of hearing, or drainage. Traumas involving the ear could include lacerations, blunt trauma and hemorrhage or bleeding in the outer ear tissue, damage from pressure changes of the ear drum (baro-trauma) from diving, high altitude, explosions or direct blows to the ear.

Earache — Pain in the ear can be associated with a number of sources, as indicated in Table 2, above. The history of trauma will be an obvious source of pain as mentioned. Most ear pain is due to an *otitis media* or infection behind the ear drum (tympanic membrane), *otitis externa* or infection in the outer ear canal (auditory canal), or due to infection

TABLE 2
Symptoms and Signs of Ear Pathology

	Hearing Loss	Pain	Head Conges- tion	Ear Drainage	Fever
Barotrauma	xx	xx		x	
Foreign Body		x		x	
Infection -					
inner ear	xx	xx	xx		xx
outer ear	x	xx		x	x
Allergy	x	x	xx		
Dental Source		x			
TMJ Source		x			
Lymph Node Source		x		x	

xx A frequent or intense symptom
x Common, less intense symptom
Blank Less likely to produce this symptom

elsewhere (generally a dental infection, infected tonsil, or lymph node in the neck near the ear). Allergy can result in pressure behind the ear drum and is also a common source of ear pain.

In the bush a simple physical examination and the additional medical history will readily (and generally accurately) distinguish the difference between an otitis media or otitis externa, and sources of pain beyond the ear. Pushing on the nob at the front of the ear (the tragus) or pulling on the ear lobe will elicit pain with an otitis externa. This will not hurt if the patient has otitis media. The history of head congestion also favors otitis media. A swollen tender nodule in the neck near the ear would be an infected lymph node. If the skin above the swelling is red, the patient probably has an infected skin abscess. The pain from an abscess is so localized, that confusion with an ear infection is seldom a problem. (Refer to section on abscess, page 96). One or more tender lymph nodes can hurt to the extent that confusion of the exact source of the pain may be in doubt. Swollen, tender lymph nodes in the neck are usually associated with *pharyngitis* or sore throat, with severe otitis externa, or with infections of the skin in the scalp. The latter should be readily noted by examination — palpate the scalp for infected cysts or abscesses. *Dental caries*, or cavities, can hurt to the extent that the pain seems to come from the ear. They can ordinarily be identified during a careful examination of the mouth. If an obvious cavity is not visualized with a light, try tapping on each tooth to see if pain is suddenly elicited. (Ref to Dental Pain, page 38).

Otitis Externa — Outer Ear Infection — This infection of the auditory canal is commonly called "swimmer's ear". The external auditory canal generally becomes inflamed from conditions of high humidity, accumulation of ear wax, or contact with contaminated water. Scratching the ear after itching the nose or scratching elsewhere may also be a source of this common infection.

Prevent cold air from blowing against the ear. Warm packs against the ear or instilling comfortably warm sweet oil can help. Provide pain medication. Obtain professional help if the patient develops a fever, the pain becomes severe, or lymph nodes or adjacent neck tissues start swelling. Significant tissue swelling will require antibiotic treatment. At times a topical will suffice, but with fever, swollen lymph or skin structures an oral antibiotic will be required.

Triple antibiotic ointment available without a prescription will work fine for outer ear infections. This is not approved by the FDA for this use, as ear infections are serious and it is not intended that non-physicians treat this condition without medical help. From the Rx kit, one should use the Neosporin ophthalmic (eye) ointment. Either ointment should be applied with the ear up and allowed to melt by body temperature. This may take 5 minutes per ear. Place cotton in the ear to hold the medication in place. Instill ointment 4 times daily and treat for 14 days. If the canal is swollen shut, a steroid ointment may also be used in between application of the other ointments just described. From the non-Rx kit use the hydrocortisone .5% cream, or from the Rx kit use Topicort .25%. Swollen tissue and/or fever also means that an oral antibiotic is required. From the Rx kit use the Bactrim DS 1 tablet twice daily or the doxycycline 100 mg twice daily. Provide the best pain medication that you can, from your non-Rx kit use 1 or 2 Mobigesic every four hours. From the Rx kit give Tylenol #3, 1 tablet every 4 hours as needed.

Otitis Media — Middle Ear Infection — This condition will present in a person who has sinus congestion and possibly drainage from allergy or infection. The ear pain can be excruciating. Fever will frequently be intermittent, normal at one moment and over 103 F at other times. Fever indicates bacterial infection of the fluid trapped behind the ear drum. If the ear drum ruptures, the pain will cease immediately and the fever will drop. This drainage allows the body to cure the infection, but will result in at least temporary damage to the ear drum and decreased hearing until it heals. There is no pain when pulling on the ear lobe or pushing on the tragus with this condition, unless an outer ear infection is also present. When visualized with an otoscope, the ear drum will be red and frequently bulging out from pressure or sucked back by a vacuum in the middle ear.

Many people will complain of hearing loss and think they have wax or a foreign body in the ear canal, when they actually have fluid accumulation behind the ear drum. Ear drops and washing the ear will not help improve this condition. Beside pain, the key to the diagnosis is head congestion and fever. There is little that can be accomplished without medication. Protect the ear from cold, position the head so that the ear is directed upwards, and provide warm packs to the ear. While drops do not help cure this problem, some pain relief may be obtained with warmed sweet oil drops in the ear.

Treatment will consist of providing decongestant, pain medication and oral antibiotic. The decongestant is Actifed, 1 tablet 4 times daily. The pain medication is given as needed as indicated in the previous section. Only the Rx Oral/Topical Unit has the proper antibiotics to treat this condition.. Use Bactrim DS 1 tablet twice daily or doxycycline 1 tablet twice daily for 5 to 7 days.

If the pressure causes the ear drum to rupture, the pain and fever will cease, but there will be a bloody drainage from the ear. Hearing is always decreased with the infection and will remain decreased due to the ruptured ear drum for some time. This generally heals itself quite well, but treat with decongestant to decrease the drainage and allow the ear drum to heal. Avoid placing drops or ointments in the ear canal if there is a chance that the ear drum has ruptured, as many medications are damaging to the inner ear mechanisms.

Foreign Body in the Ear — These are generally of three types. Accumulation of wax plugs (cerumen), foreign objects, and living insects. Wax plugs can usually be softened with a warmed oil. This may have to be placed in the ear canal repeatedly over many days. Irrigating with room temperature water may be attempted with a bulb syringe, such as the one recommended for wound irrigation in the Field Surgical Unit. If a wax plugged ear becomes painful, treat as indicated in the section on otitis externa.

The danger in trying to remove inanimate objects is the tendency to shove them further into the ear canal or to damage the delicate ear canal lining, thus adding bleeding to your troubles. Of course, rupturing the ear drum by shoving against it would be a real unnecessary disaster. Attempt to grasp a foreign body with a pair of tweezers if you can visualize it. Do not poke blindly with anything. Irrigation may be attempted as indicated above.

A popular method of aiding in the management of insects in the ear canal is the instillation of lidocaine to kill the bug instantly prior to attempting removal. There are reports of lidocaine making a person very dizzy, especially if some leaks through a hole in the ear drum into the inner ear. This dizziness will be very distressing if it happens and can result in profound vomiting and discomfort should it occur. It is self limiting and should last not more than a day if it does transpire. An alternate method is to drown the bug with cooking or other oil, then attempt removal. Oil seems to kill bugs quicker than water. The less struggle, the less chance for stinging, biting, or other trauma to the delicate ear canal and ear drum. Tilt the ear downward, thus hoping to slide the dead bug towards the entrance where it can be grappled. Shining a light at the ear to coax a bug out is probably futile.

TMJ Syndrome — The temporal-mandibular joint is the hinge joint of the jaw. You can easily feel it move if you place a finger tip into your ear canal. If this joint becomes irritated, it will frequently cause ear pain. It will generally be painful to push directly on this joint, which is located just forward of the ear. No swelling should be noted. Tenderness is increased with chewing, and pain and popping or locking may be noted when opening the jaw widely.

Treatment is with local heat. The use of aspirin or Mobigesic can be very helpful. At times Tylenol #3 may be required. Do not eat foods that are hard to chew or which require opening the mouth widely.

Ruptured Ear Drum — This can result from direct puncture, from explosions, and from barotrauma of diving deep or of high altitude. Being smacked on the ear can also rupture the ear drum.

Avoid diving or rapid ascents of altitude in vehicles or airplanes if suffering from sinus congestion. Congestion can lead to blockage of the eustachian tube. Failure to equilibrate pressure through this tube between the middle ear and the throat — and thus the outside world — can result in damage to the ear drum. In case of congestion, take a decongestant such as Actifed 1 tablet every 4 hours until clear. Cancel any plans of diving if congested. Also, if a gradual pressure squeeze is causing pain while diving, the dive should be terminated.

When flying, it will be noted that blocked eustachian tubes will cause more pain upon descent than ascent. When going up the pressure in the inner ear will increase and blow out through the eustachian tube. When coming down increased outer atmospheric pressure is much less apt to clear the plugged tube and a squeeze of air against the ear drum will result. Try to equalize this pressure by pinching the nose shut and gently increasing the pressure in your mouth and throat against closed lips.

This will generally clear the eustachian tube and relieve the air squeeze on the ear drum. Do not over-do this; that can also be painful. If barotrauma results in ear drum rupture, the pain should instantly cease. There may be bloody drainage from the ear canal. Do not place drops in the ear canal, but drainage can be gently wiped away or frequently changed cotton plugs used to catch the bloody fluid.

SORE THROAT — The most common cause of a sore throat, or pharyngitis, is a viral infection. While uncomfortable, this malady requires no antibiotic treatment — in fact, antibiotics will do no good whatsoever. Strictly speaking, the sore throat that needs to be treated is the one caused by a specific bacteria (beta hemolytic streptococcus, Lancefield group A) as it has been found that treatment for ten days will avoid the dreaded complication of rheumatic fever which may occur in 1% to 3% of the people who contract this particular infection. Many purists in the medical profession feel that no antibiotics should be used until the results of a throat culture or antibody screen proving this particular infection have been returned from the lab. On a short trip the victim can be taken to a doctor for a strep culture to determine if the sore throat was indeed strep. On a wilderness trip longer than 2 weeks, it would be best to commit the patient to a 10 day therapy of antibiotic, realizing that the symptoms will soon pass and the patient seem well, but that it is essential to continue the medication for 10 days.

There are text book differences in the general appearance of a viral and strep sore throat. The lymph nodes in the neck are swollen in both cases, they are more tender with bacterial infections, but people with a low pain threshold will complain bitterly about soreness regardless of the source of infection. The throat will be quite red in bacterial infection and a white splotchy coating over the red tonsils or back portion of the throat generally means a bacterial infection — at least these classic indications are present 20% of the time. Sore throats caused by some viral infections (namely infectious mononucleosis and adenovirus) may mimic all of the above. While the ideal antibiotic for strep throat is penicillin, from the suggested Rx kit you will have to use doxycycline 100 mg twice daily for 10 days.

INFECTIOUS MONONUCLEOSIS — This disease of young adults (teens through 30 years of age), generally presents as a terrible sore throat, swollen lymph nodes (normally at the back of the neck and not as tender as with strep infection), and a profound tired feeling. This disease is self-limited with total recovery to be expected after 2 weeks for most victims — some, unfortunately are bed-ridden for weeks and lethargic for 6 months. Spleen enlargement is common. The most serious aspect of this disease is the possibility of splenic rupture, but this is rare. Avoid palpating the spleen (ie shoving on the left upper quadrant of the abdomen), let the victim *rest* — no hiking, etc., until the illness and feeling of lethargy has passed. The first five days are the worst, with fever and excruciating sore throat being the major complaint.

Treatment is symptomatic with medication for fever and pain such as the Non-Rx Mobigesic 1 or 2 tablets every 4 to 6 hours, or the Rx Tylenol #3 1 or 2 tablets every 4 to 6 hours. A mild form of hepatitis frequently occurs with mononucleosis that causes nausea and loss of appetite. This requires no specific treatment other than rest. If severe ear pain begins, add a decongestant such as Actifed 1 tablet every 6 hours to promote relief of eustachian tube pressure. Due to the uncertainty of diagnosis, treat the severe sore throat as if it were a strep infection with antibiotic for 10 days as indicated in the section on sore throat above.

DENTAL PAIN — Cavities may be identified by visual examination of the mouth in most cases. At times the pain is so severe that the patient cannot tell exactly which tooth is the offender. A painful tooth will not refer pain to the opposite side of the mouth. Painful back teeth normally do not refer pain to front teeth and vice-versa. With the painful area narrowed down, look for an obvious cavity. If none is found, tap each tooth in turn until the offending one is reached — a tap on it will elicit strong pain.

Dry the tooth and try to clean out any cavity found. For years oil of cloves, or eugenol, has been used to deaden dental pain. Avoid trying to apply an aspirin directly to a painful tooth, it will only make a worse mess of things. Many excellent dental kits are now available without prescription that contain topical anesthetic agents and temporary fillings. Lacking this, a daub of topical anesthetic such as the 1% Dibucaine ointment will work. Before applying the anesthetic, dry the tooth and try to clean out any cavity found. From the Rx kit, Tylenol #3 1 or 2 tabs every 4 hours will generally eliminate the most severe dental pain. Or from the non-Rx kit, give Mobigesic 2 tabs every 4 hours for pain. When in the bush and a tooth ache begins, I would also start treating with an antibiotic if the Rx kit is available. The drug of choice for this problem is penicillin 250 mg 4 times daily for 10 days or erythromycin 250 mg 4 times daily for 10 days, but they have not been included in the Rx Oral/Topical Unit. Excellent alternatives are listed, however, and you may give doxycycline 100 mg twice daily, or the Bactrim DS twice daily.

SWOLLEN, PAINFUL GUMS — Pain attended by swelling high up the gum at the base of the tooth, usually indicates an infection and a tooth that may require extraction, or root canal therapy if a dentist can be consulted who has brought more than just his fly rod with him on the trip. Attempting to avoid either, have the patient use warm water mouth rinses. Start the victim on antibiotics as indicated in the previous section. If a bulging area can be identified in the mouth, an incision with a #11 scalpel blade may promote drainage. If the pain is severe and not relieved with the Tylenol #3, the tooth may have to be pulled.

Swelling at the gum line, rather than at the base of the tooth, may indicate a periodontal abscess. The gingiva (or gums) are red, swollen, foul smelling and oozing. Frequently this represents food particle entrapment and abscess formation along the surface of the tooth with the gums — the so-called gingival cuff. Considerable relief can often be obtained by probing directly into the abscess area through the gingival cuff, using any thin, blunt instrument. Probe along the length of the tooth to break up and drain the abscess. Have the patient use frequent hot mouth rinses to continue the drainage process. If a foreign object, such as a piece of food, is causing the swelling, irrigate with warm salt solution or warm water, with sufficient force to dislodge the particle. Probe it loose if necessary. Dental floss may be very helpful.

Acute pain and swelling of the tissue behind the third molar usually represents an erupting wisdom tooth. Technically this is called "pericoronitis." There is a little flap of tissue that lies over the erupting wisdom tooth called the "operculum." Biting on this causes it to swell, and then it becomes much easier to bite on it again, and so on... The end result is considerable pain. This can be relieved by surgically removing the operculum. If local anesthetic is available, such as lidocaine, inject it directly into the operculum and then cut it out with a scalpel blade using the outline of the erupting tooth as a guideline. The bleeding can soon be stopped by biting down on a gauze or other cloth after the procedure is over. Stitching this wound is not required. If no lidocaine is available, swab the area with alcohol as this helps provide some slight anesthesia. Application of topical anesthetic, especially saliva resistant, may also be of slight help.

Swelling of the entire side of the face will occur with dental infections that spread. *This condition should ideally be treated in a hospital setting with intravenous antibiotics.* In the bush, apply warm compresses to the face and give antibiotic coverage as indicated in the section on dental pain. Do not lance these from the skin side, but a peaked, bulging area on the inside of the mouth may be lanced to promote drainage. Abscess extension into surrounding facial tissues generally means that lancing will do little good. This patient is very ill and rest is mandatory.

Provide antibiotic coverage as indicated in the previous section.

MOUTH SORES — When these develop the two concerns that the patient frequently has is the possibility of cancer or infection, especially herpes. A common reason for a lesion is the sore called a papilloma caused from rubbing against a sharp tooth or dental work. They can look serious, but are not. They are raised, normally orange in color. Usually one can find an obvious rough area causing the irritation. Treatment is to avoid chewing at the lesion, apply eugenol or other anesthetic agent, or ideally Kenalog in orabase from the Rx kit, every 3 hours.

A canker sore, also called an aphthous ulcer, can appear anywhere in the mouth and be any size. It has a distinctive appearance of a white crater with a red, swollen border. Treatment is as above.

If there is generalized tissue swelling, possibly drainage or whitish cover on the gums, the breath is foul smelling and the gums and tissue of the mouth bleed easily when scraped, it is possible that the victim has trench mouth or Vincent's infection. This is caused by poor hygiene, which is unfortunately common on long expeditions under adverse circumstances. If the white exudate is located over the tonsils, one has to consider strep throat (see page 37), mononucleosis (see page 37), and diphtheria. Treat trench mouth with warm water rinses, swishing the crude off as well as possible. If the Rx kit is available, give doxycycline 100 mg twice daily for 4 to 5 days.

The mouth lesions of herpes simplex begin as small blisters that leave a raw area once they have broken open. The ulceration from a herpes is red rather than the white of the canker sore. They are very painful. While Zovirax ointment is the Rx drug of choice, application of topical anesthetic such as the Non-Rx dibucaine ointment will provide pain relief for the 10 days or so that the lesions are active. Application of the Rx Kenalog in orabase relieves the inflammation rapidly. Zovirax has not been recommended for inclusion in the Wilderness Medical Kit modules, but if you are bothered with this problem frequently, consider including it.

LACERATIONS OF MOUTH — Any significant trauma to the mouth causes considerable bleeding and concern. The bleeding initially always seems worse than it is. Rinse the mouth with warm water to clear away the clots so that you can tell where the bleeding has been coming from.

Laceration of the piece of tissue that seems to join the bottom lip or upper lip to the gum line is a common result of trauma to the mouth and need not be repaired, even though it initially looks horrible and may bleed considerably. This is called the labial frenum. Simply stuff some gauze into the area until the bleeding stops.

A laceration of the tongue will not require stitching (suturing) unless an edge is deeply involved. Fairly deep cuts along the top surface and bottom can be ignored in the wilderness setting.If suturing is to be accomplished and you have injectable lidocaine from the Rx kit, inject into the lower gum behind the teeth on the side of the gum facing the tongue. Technically this area is called the median raphe distal to the posterior teeth. This will block the side of the tongue and be much less painful than directly injecting into the tongue. Use the 3-0 gut sutures. These sutures will dissolve within a few days. Sutures in the tongue frequently come out within a few hours, even when they are well tied, much to the victim and surgeon's annoyance. If this happens and the tongue is not bleeding badly, just leave it alone. Minor cuts along the edge of the tongue can also be ignored.

Make sure that cuts on the inside of the mouth do not have foreign bodies, such as pieces of tooth inside of them. These must be removed. Inject the lidocaine into the wound before probing if you have the Rx Injectable Medication Unit. Irrigate thoroughly with water. Even without the lidocaine, the inside of the mouth can be stitched with minimal pain. Use the 3-0 gut suture, removing them in 4 days if the suture has not fallen out already. Refer to page 92 for discussion of suturing the face and outside of the lips.

LOST FILLING — This could turn into a real disaster. An old fashion remedy was to use powdered zinc oxide (not the ointment) and eugenol. Starting with the two in equal parts, mix until a putty is formed by adding more zinc oxide powder as necessary. This always takes considerably more of the zinc oxide than at first would seem necessary. Pack this putty into the cavity and allow to set over the next 24 hours.

The Cavit dental filling paste in the Rx Oral/Topical Unit provides a strong temporary filling. Dry the cavity bed thoroughly with a gauze square. Place several drops of anesthetic, such as the oil of cloves (eugenol), to deaden the nerve endings and kill bacteria. Dibucaine ointment from the Non-Rx Oral/Topical Unit can be used for this purpose. You will have to pack the ointment into the cavity area and allow it to melt. Dry the cavity carefully once again. The Cavit paste should be applied to the dry cavity and packed firmly into place.

Obviously avoid biting on the side of the filling, regardless of the materials used to make your temporary filling. See a dentist as soon as possible as the loss of a filling may indicate extension of decay in the underlying tooth.

LOOSE TOOTH — When you examine a traumatized mouth and find a tooth that is rotated, or dislocated in any direction, do not push the tooth back into place. Further movement may disrupt the tooth's blood and nerve supply. If the tooth is at all secure leave it alone. The musculature of the lips and tongue will generally and gently push the tooth back into place and keep it there.

A fractured tooth with exposed pink substance that is bleeding, is showing exposed nerve. This tooth will need protection with eugenol and temporary filling as indicated above. This is actually a dental emergency that should be treated by a dentist immediately.

If a tooth is knocked out, replace it into the socket immediately. If this cannot be done, have the victim hold the tooth under their tongue or in their lower lip until it can be implanted. In any case hours is a matter of great importance. A tooth left out too long will be rejected by the body as a foreign substance.

All of the above problems will mean that a soft diet and avoidance of chewing with the affected tooth for many days will be necessary. In the wilderness setting, start the patient on antibiotic such as the doxycycline 100 mg, 1 daily for any of the above problems.

Trauma that can cause any of the above may also result in fractures of the tooth below the gum line or of the alveolar ridge affecting several teeth. If this is suspected, start the patient on antibiotic as mentioned in the paragraph above. Oral surgical help must be obtained as soon as possible. A soft diet is essential until healing takes place, possibly a matter of 6 to 8 weeks.

PULLING A TOOTH — It is best not to pull a tooth from an infected gum as this might spread the infection. If an abscess is forming, place the patient on antibiotic, such as the doxycycline 100 mg twice daily, and use warm mouth rinses to promote drainage. After the infection has subsided it will be safer to pull the tooth. Opening the abscess as described in that section will be helpful at times. If it appears necessary to pull an infected tooth, give the patient an antibiotic pill about 2 hours before pulling the tooth to provide some protection against spreading the infection.

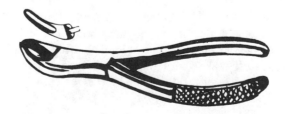

FIGURE 7. UNIVERSAL DENTAL EXTRACTION FORCEPS

Pull the tooth by obtaining a secure hold with the universal dental extraction forceps (figure 7). Slowly apply pressure in a back-and-forth, side-to-side motion to rock the tooth free. This loosens the tooth in its socket and will permit its removal. Avoid jerking or pulling the tooth with a straight outward force; it can resist all of the strength that you have in this direction. Jerking may break off the root.

If the root breaks off, you may leave it alone rather than trying to dig it out. If the root section is obviously loose, then you can pick it out with some suitable instrument. Thin fragments of bone may fracture off during the extraction. These will work their way to the surface during healing. Do not attempt to replace them, but pick them free as they surface.

If you do not have dental forceps, it is best to not attempt to pull the tooth with another instrument. Pliers may crush the tooth and the tooth will slip in your grasp. A large, solid tooth can be removed by using your finger to rock it back and forth. This may take days to accomplish, but it will eventually loosen sufficiently to remove.

FRICTION BLISTERS — A relatively new and easily obtainable substance has revolutionized the prevention and care of friction blisters. The substance is Spenco 2nd Skin, available at most athletic supply and drug stores. Made from an inert, breathable gel consisting of 4% polyethylene oxide and 96% water, it has the feel and consistency of, well most people would say snot. It comes in various sized sheets, sterile, and sealed in water-tight packages. It is very cool to the touch, in fact large sheets are sold to cover infants to reduce a fever. It has three valuable properties that make it so useful. One, it will remove all friction between two moving surfaces (hence its use in prevention) and two, it cleans and deodorizes wounds by absorbing blood, serum, or pus. Three, its cooling effect is very soothing, which aids in pain relief.

It comes between two sheets of cellophane. It must be held against the wound and for that purpose the same company produces an adhesive knit bandage. For prevention the 2nd Skin can be applied with the cellophane attached and secured with the knit bandaging. For treatment of a hot spot, remove the cellophane from one side and apply this gooey side against the wound, again securing it with the knit bandaging. If a friction blister has developed, it will have to be lanced. Cleanse with soap or surgical scrub and open along an edge with a #11 scalpel blade or equal. After expressing the fluid, apply a fully stripped piece of 2nd Skin. This is easiest done by removing the cellophane from one side, then applying it to the wound. Once on the skin surface, remove the cellophane from the outside edge. Over this you will need to place the adhesive knit. The bandage must be kept moist with clean water. Applied through the adhesive knit, routine moistening will allow the same bandage to be used for days or until the wound is healed.

Unless you have a friction blister and try using this stuff, you'll find it hard to believe how well it works!

THERMAL BURNS — As soon as possible remove the source of the burn — quick immersion into cool water will help eliminate additional heat from scalding water or burning fuels and clothing. Or otherwise suffocate the flames with clothing, sand, etc. Running will fan flames and increase the injury.

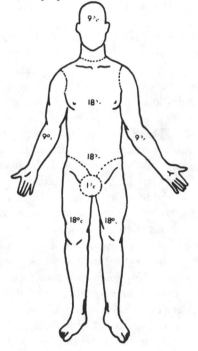

FIGURE 8. "RULE OF NINES" BURN CHART

Treatment of burns depends upon the extent (percent of the body covered) and the severity (degree) of the injury. The percent of the body covered is estimated by referring to the Rule of Nines, as indicated in figure 8. An entire arm equals 9% of the body surface area, therefore the burn of just one side of the forearm would equal about 2%. The chest and back equal 18% and the abdomen and back equal 18%. The proportions are slightly different for children.

Severity of burns is indicated by degree. First Degree (superficial) will have redness and be dry and painful. Second Degree (partial skin thickness) will be moist, painful, and have bleb formation with reddened bases. Third Degree (deep) involves the full thickness of the skin and extends into the subcutaneous tissue with char, loss of substance, or discoloration. These are frequently not painful due to nerve destruction, although there will be painful lesions of second and first degree burn surrounding the area.

The field treatment of burns has been revolutionized by the development of Spenco 2nd Skin. It is the perfect substance to use on 1st, 2nd, or 3rd degree burns. Its cooling effect relieves pain, while its sterile covering absorbs fluid easily from the wound. If applied to a charred 3rd degree burn, it provides a sterile cover that does not have to be changed. If the patient arrives at a hospital, it can easily be removed in a whirlpool bath. For details on application technique, refer to the section on friction blisters.

For purposes of field management, victims can be divided into three groups depending upon a combination of the extent and severity of the burn.

First and second degree burns involving less than 15% of an adult (10% of a child) — Cleanse the area with non-medicated soap and water and rinse thoroughly. All grease and foreign material should be removed. First degree burns may be covered with 1% dibucaine ointment from the non-Rx kit, which should provide almost complete pain relief. An alternate dressing would be the application of Spenco 2nd Skin for its soothing relief. Large blisters may be lanced and the collapsed skin allowed to cover the wound. Spenco 2nd Skin application will protect the wound and allow seepage of fluid. Remove both coverings of cellophane and hold in place with the adhesive knit covering. This dressing should be kept damp with sterile water. First degree burns will heal in 3 days. Second degree burns may take up to 2 weeks. The Spenco dressing may be left in position until healing is completed.

Second degree burns will slough the skin after 3 to 4 days. The skin appears white and frequently an ooze of pus may develop. If the underlying skin does not become red and swollen, then this is a normal development. As mentioned, healing will take place in 2 weeks. The dead skin can be cut away or left to dry out and slough off on its own. These changes will not be as noticeable if the 2nd Skin is left in place during this entire time. Red swollen skin may indicate an infection. In this case, provide antibiotic from the Rx kit such as doxycycline 100 mg twice daily or Bactrim DS twice daily. If no antibiotic is available, promote localization by the application of warm compresses for 20 minutes, every 2 hours and cover with triple antibiotic ointment from the non-Rx kit.

Pain medication will be required for either burn. From the non-Rx kit give Mobigesic, 1 or 2 tablets every 4 hours as required, or from the Rx kit provide Tylenol #3 1 or 2 tablets every 4 hours as required.

Third degree burns involving less than 15% of an adult (10% of a child) and deep second degree burns, except on face and hands — Generally these patients will not require treatment for shock. Management of the actual burn is as outlined above. A third degree burn of more than 1/2 square inch will require eventual skin graft. In the meantime, the Spenco 2nd Skin will make the ideal dressing. Treat infection and pain as indicated in the section above.

Third degree and extensive second degree burns involving more than 15% of an adult (10% of a child), or second degree burns on the face or hands — SHOCK SHOULD BE ANTICIPATED AND TREATMENT BEGUN IMMEDIATELY — THIS TAKES PRECEDENCE OVER WOUND CARE.

Replacement of fluid loss will be the mainstay of shock prevention. The only practical route available to most wilderness travelers will be the oral route, or by mouth. The rule of thumb is to push as much oral fluid as tolerated. Any excess will be urinated off. The amount needed will probably exceed 5 quarts during the first 8-hour period, with another 5 quarts over the next 16 hours. This volume may be adjusted depending upon the urine flow and pulse rate, the two most easily measured parameters of hypovolemic (low fluid level) shock. The ideal urine flow rate should be 50 ml to 100 ml (1 2/3 ounce to 3 1/3 ounce) per hour. The pulse rate will be elevated due to pain, but it is still a good indicator of hypovolemic conditions and their correction. In adults the rate should be less than 140/min.; in children less than 180/min. If a blood pressure cuff is available — a normal or high blood pressure should be maintained. The serious difficulty reached with the oral replacement technique is two-fold. The first is vomiting and the second is inability to keep up with fluid losses via the oral route alone if more than 30% of the body surface area is burned.

The replacement fluid would ideally consist of Gatorade diluted 1:1 with water or a mixture consisting of 1/3 teaspoon of salt and 1/3 teaspoon of baking soda in one quart of flavored, sweetened water. Avoid the use of potassium rich solutions (orange juice, apple juice) as red blood cell destruction will be raising serum potassium to high levels during the first 24 hours.

Generally patients with less than 20% of their body surface area burned can tolerate fluids very well. If they are not vomiting, those with between 20% and 30% of their body surface area involved can be resuscitated by this method without the need for IV fluid replacement, but the patient will have to be treated for shock with the body placed in a recumbent position — feet elevated. This individual will certainly be marginally shocky. If the victim is vomiting, he will fall way behind in fluid replacement.

During the second day, the oral fluids may consist of diluted Gatorade and sweetened, flavored water (such as Wylers). Watch urine flow to determine the amount of fluids required. On the third day, the patient should be given a moderately high carbohydrate diet, rich in protein. Approximately 200 mg of Vitamin C and substantial Vitamin B complex should be given per day. This would equal about 4 each One-A-Day multiple Vitamin (Miles) or equivalent. Avoid an excessive amount of carbohydrate during the first few days, as a fatal diabetes may result.

Relieve pain with 2 Mobigesic every 4 hours from the non-Rx kit or 1 or 2 Tylenol #3 from the Rx kit as needed. If you have the Rx Injectable Module, you may give 10 mg Nubain IM every 4 to 6 hours as needed for pain and/or 25 mg of Vistaril IM every 4 hours for nausea. Avoid the use of oral antibiotics to prevent wound infection. If an infection develops, then you may start what you have available, namely from the Rx kit doxycycline 100 mg twice daily or Bactrim DS twice daily. Spenco 2nd Skin is the ideal burn dressing for these severe burns. It provides a breathable cover that is sterile and which will exclude bacteria from the environment. It is also easily removable with whirlpool or gentle cleansing in the hospital. A topical antibiotic ointment may be applied such as the triple antibiotic ointment.

Occlusive dressings must not be used. The ointment may be placed on thick gauze dressings which are then held against the wound with a single layer of gauze roll dressing. The wound should be cleaned daily, removing dead tissue. This can be done with gentle scraping using sterile gauze and clean water with a little Hibiclens surgical scrub added, after proper pain medication has been provided. These patients must obviously be evacuated as soon as possible.

IV fluid replacement would, of course, require sterile needle, IV tubing administration set, and IV fluids. The IV fluid for the first 24 hours should consist solely of Ringer's lactate in an amount calculated by multiplying the patient's weight in kilograms times the total percent of the body surface area burned — not a maximum of 50% as many formulae have previously recommended. Prior to 24 hours post burn, the capillary leakage of plasma will make use of this substance ineffective — a tolerable equilibrium will be established. The essential management during that first 24 hours is adequate Ringer's lactate replacement. Since each liter of Ringer's lactate contains 75 ml to 100 ml of free water, it is also not necessary to add D5W during that first day. During the fourth 8 hour period (24 hour to 32 hour post-burn), plasma expansion should be completely provided. The amount of plasma depends upon the extent of the burn.

% burn	Plasma Required for 155 pound man
20 to 40	0 to 500 ml
40 to 60	500 to 1700 ml
60 to 80	1000 to 3000 ml
greater than 80	1500 to 3500 ml

Following the administration of the above, no further volume expansion will normally be required. The daily insensible water losses will have to be replaced. Generally this can revert to the oral (by mouth) replacement method. Due to increased insensible loss through burned skin, this amount should be increased to 3 quarts per day (see further discussion in section on WATER CONSUMPTION, Page 70. It should be obvious from the above, that the wilderness medic, without aid of IV fluids and equipment and without proper sterile environment, has little chance of saving a victim with greater than 30% body burns, that 20% to 30% burn victims have a marginal chance, primarily dependent upon the amount of vomiting, while victims with less than 15% burn, 1° and 2°, should fare well. If limited IV solutions are to be carried, the ideal would be Ringer's lactate in collapsible bags. Plasma comes in glass bottles and cost about $100 per bottle. Refrigeration is not required.

DIABETES MANAGEMENT — A diabetic child or adult can have an active outdoor life, but first learning to control their diabetes is an essential process to be worked out between that individual and their physician. The increased caloric requirement of wilderness exercise may range to an extra 2,000 calories per day, yet insulin dosage requirements may drop as much as 50%. The diabetic and trip partners must be able to identify the signs of low blood sugar (hypoglycemia) — staggering gait, slurred speech, moist skin, clumsy movements — and know the proper treatment, i.e. oral carbohydrates or sugar candies and the use of injectable glucagon (if the patient becomes unconscious). Urine of diabetic outdoor travelers should be tested twice daily to confirm control of sugar. This testing should preclude a gradual accumulation of too much blood sugar, which can result in unconsciousness in its far advanced stage. This gradual accumulation would have resulted in massive sugar spill in the urine, and finally the spill of ketone bodies, providing the patient ample time to increase insulin dosage to prevent hyperglycemia (too high a blood sugar level).

Storage of insulin in the wilderness, where it foregoes recommended refrigeration, is not a major problem so long as the supply is fresh and direct sunlight and excessive heat is avoided. Syringes, alcohol prep pads, Keto-diastix urine test strips, insulin and glucagon are light additions to the wilderness medical kit.

DIFFICULTY BREATHING —
If no breathing is present — from whatever cause —
  refer to **RESCUE BREATHING,** Page 49.
If no heart beat is present — from whatever cause —
  refer to **CARDIAC COMPRESSION,** Page 50.
If the difficulty starts at high altitude (above 6,500 feet),
  refer to the section on **HIGH ALTITUDE ILLNESS,** Page 59.
If the difficulty starts under cold conditions, or conditions of cold weather exposure (under 45°F),
  refer to **HYPOTHERMIA,** Page 62.
If body oral temperature is over 100°F and cough is present —
  refer to **PNEUMONIA/BRONCHITIS,** Page 56.
If pain is of sudden onset, for no apparent reason, pain in one area made worse with breathing —
  refer to **PNEUMOTHORAX,**Page 56.
If associated with pressure feeling, or ache in middle chest, possibly radiating into neck or arm, made worse with exertion and easing with rest; patient sweating, no temp —
  refer to **CARDIAC,** Page 50-52.

RESCUE BREATHING — New techniques for rescue breathing were established in 1986. The best way to provide artificial respiration is by using the mouth-to-mouth technique. The victim should be touched on the shoulder to make sure that he is unconscious. If the victim is not lying flat on his back, roll him over, moving the entire body at one time as a total unit. The rescuer should place his face near the victim's to ascertain whether or not air movement is occurring through the mouth or nose. If breathing is absent, the oropharynx and mouth should be cleared of foreign material (snow, mucus, dental plates, vomit, etc.) by inserting the fingers into the mouth and scooping this material out. To open the victim's airway, use the head-tilt/chin-lift method, rather than the head-tilt/neck-lift method as taught before 1986. Place one hand on the victim's forehead and apply firm, backwards pressure with the palm to tilt the head back. Also place the fingers of the other hand under the boney part of the lower jaw near the chin and lift to bring the chin forward and the teeth almost shut, thus supporting the jaw and helping to tilt the head back, as indicated in figure 9. In case of suspected neck injury, use the chin-lift without the head-tilt technique. The nose is pinched shut by using the thumb and index finger of the hand on the forehead.

FIGURE 9. HEAD TILT/CHIN LIFT METHOD OF OPENING THE AIR WAY IN AN UNCONSCIOUS PERSON

The chin-lift method will place tension on the tongue and throat structures to insure that the air passage will open. This opening of the air passage may be all that is required to allow the victim to start breathing again. Reassess breathing again by looking for the chest raising or falling, listening for air escaping during expiration, and feeling the movement of air.

Give two initial breaths of 1 to 1 1/2 seconds each, as opposed to the "4 quick breaths" previously recommended. The rescuer should take a breath after each ventilation. If the initial attempt to ventilate does not work, reposition the victim's head and try again. If ventilation still does not work, proceed with foreign-body airway obstruction maneuvers. If it does work, assess circulatory status and provide cardiac compressions if necessary. If pulses can be felt, but the patient is not breathing on his own, continue mouth-to-mouth ventilation at the rate of 12 breaths per minute. THE ONLY WAY TO LEARN THIS TECHNIQUE IS TO TAKE A CPR COURSE — IT CANNOT BE PROPERLY SELF-TAUGHT.

CARDIAC COMPRESSION — Check the victim's carotid pulse. This is easily found by placing your hand on the voice box (larynx). Slide the tips of your fingers into the groove beside the voice box and feel for the pulse — this is where the carotid artery can easily be palpated. If the pulse cannot be felt, the rescuer must provide artificial circulation in addition to artificial respiration. This is best done with external cardiac compression (see *Figure 10a&b*). Kneel at the victim's side near his chest, locating the notch at the lowest portion of his sternum. Place the heel of one hand on the sternum 1 1/2 to 2 inches above this notch. Place the other hand on top of the one that is in position and the sternum. Be sure to keep your fingers off the ribs. The easiest way to prevent this is to interlock your fingers, thus keeping them confined to the sternum. With your shoulders directly over the victim's sternum, compress downward keeping your arms straight. Depress the sternum 1 1/2 to 2 inches for an average adult victim. Relax the pressure completely, keeping your hands in contact with the sternum at all times, but allowing the sternum to return to its normal position between compressions. Both compression and relaxation should be of equal duration. Perform 15 external chest compressions at a rate of 80 to 100 per minute. Open the airway and deliver 2 rescue breaths. Locate the proper hand position and begin 15 more compressions at a rate of 80 to 100 per minute. Perform 4 complete cycles of 15 compressions and 2 ventilations.

After 4 cycles of compressions and ventilations (15:2 ration), reevaluate the patient. Check for the return of the carotid pulse (5 seconds). If it is absent, resume CPR with 2 ventilations followed by compressions. If it is present, continue to the next step.

Check breathing (3 to 5 seconds). If present, monitor breathing and pulse closely. If absent, perform rescue breathing at 12 times per minute and monitor pulse closely.

If CPR is continued, stop and check for return of pulse and spontaneous breathng every few minutes. Do not interrupt CPR for more than 7 seconds except in special circumstances.

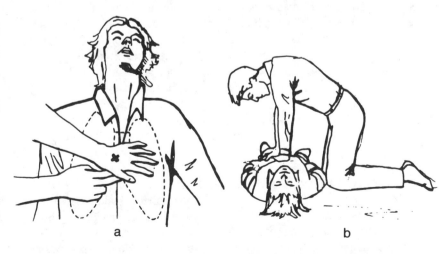

a   b

FIGURE 10A. CPR —   FIGURE 10B. CPR —
POSITION OF HANDS   POSITION OF RESCUER

Once CPR is started it should be maintained until professional assistance can take over the responsibility, or until a physician declares the patient dead. If CPR has been continued for 30 minutes without regaining cardiac function, and the eyes are fixed and non-reactive to light, the patient can be presumed dead. The exceptions would be hypothermia (see page 62) and lightning injuries (page 57). In these circumstances CPR should be continued until the rescuers are exhausted if professional help does not intervene.

Some authorities in wilderness rescue have felt that the survival rate is so low without defibrillation within 4 minutes by paramedics, that CPR should not be started in the bush when cardiac standstill is due to a heart attack. It certainly should not be started or maintained under these conditions when its performance might endanger the lives of members of the rescue party. Regardless, learning CPR is an important skill that every person should master. THE ONLY WAY TO LEARN THIS TECHNIQUE IS TO TAKE A CPR COURSE — IT CANNOT BE PROPERLY SELF-TAUGHT.

MYOCARDIAL INFARCTION — HEART ATTACK — The symptoms of chest heaviness or pain with exertion; pain or ache radiating into the neck or into the arms; sweating, clammy, pale appearance; shortness of breath — are fairly classic for a cardiac victim. The only thing which can be done for this individual is rest. Position the victim for optimum comfort, generally with his head elevated about 45 degrees. In some cases, even with an electrocardiogram, it is impossible for a trained physician to determine whether or not an individual is having a cardiac problem. When in doubt — rest the patient and try to evacuate without having him do any of the work. *Treat as a total invalid.* You may give the victim Tylenol #3 for pain and Atarax 25 mg to prevent nausea and to help sedate the victim. If pain is severe give 2 of the Tylenol #3. You may repeat the pain medication every 3 to 4 hours and the nausea/sedation medication every 4 hours as needed. If you have the Rx Injectable Module, you may give 10 mg Nubain IM every 4 to 6 hours as needed for pain and/or 25 mg of Vistaril IM every 4 hours for nausea.

FOREIGN-BODY AIRWAY OBSTRUCTION MANEUVERS — The subdiaphragmatic abdominal thrust, also called "Abdominal thrust" or "Heimlich Maneuver", is recommended for relieving foreign-body airway obstruction, or choking. If the victim is standing or sitting, the rescuer stands behind and wraps his arms around the patient, proceeding as follows: Make a fist with one hand. Place the thumb side of the fist against the victim's abdomen, in the midline slightly above the navel and well below the breast bone (xiphoid process of the sternum). Grasp the fist with the other hand. Press the fist into the victim's abdomen with a quick upward thrust. Each new thrust should be a separate and distinct movement. It may be necessary to repeat the thrust 6 to 10 times to clear the airway.

If the victim is unconscious or on the ground, the victim should be placed on his back face up. The rescuer kneels astride the victim's thighs. The rescuer places the heel of one hand against the victim's abdomen, in the midline slightly above the navel and well below the breast bone, and the second hand directly on top of the first. The rescuer then presses into the abdomen with a quick upward thrust.

Were these maneuvers to fail with the debris located above the trachea, a tracheostomy would be life saving. Probably the best field expedient technique is the cricothyrotomy.

CRICOTHYROTOMY — If the patient is in imminent danger of dying from airway obstruction, the obstruction or damage being at a level of the larynx or above, a rapid field technique to provide an artificial airway that is very dangerous, but less so than the even more dangerous tracheostomy, is the cricothyrotomy. In essence, a hole is placed in the thin cricothyroid membrane and a hollow object is placed in this hole to keep an external airway open. This membrane stretches between the Adam's apple (thyroid cartilage) and the prominent ring just below the Adam's apple, called the cricoid cartilage.

With the patient lying on a flat surface, head extended, prepare the area with antiseptic if there is time. Povidine-iodine or alcohol prep pads would work well. Palpate for the cricothyroid membrane's location between the Adam's apple and cricoid cartilage. Make a vertical stab incision through the outer skin and the membrane. This opening will have to be kept from collapsing with the use of a hollow tube (such as a ball point pen casing, if nothing better is available.) [A cannula made especially for this purpose is manufactured by Becton-Dickenson, the Adelson curved cricothyroidotomy cannula, and can be ordered by your physician through a surgical supply house.] This cannula would be anchored in place as per the instructions which come with the device. Any large bore needle may be used (12 or 14 gauge — the lower the number, the larger the needle bore.) After placement, the needle would have to be carefully taped into position to prevent dislodgement (see *Figure 11*). Two needles can be placed side by side to provide better ventilation, especially if oxygen is not available to enrich the mixture the patient is breathing.

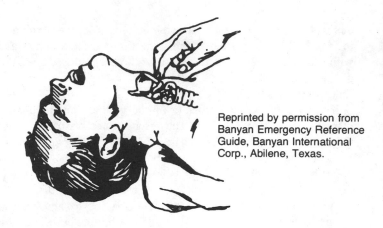

Reprinted by permission from
Banyan Emergency Reference
Guide, Banyan International
Corp., Abilene, Texas.

FIGURE 11. PALPATION OF THE CRICOID MEMBRANE

There are many complications that can result from this procedure —
the esophagus can be punctured, the cricoid cartilage and first tracheal
ring may be cut, the recurrent laryngeal nerve may be cut, causing
damage to the voice, and even the top of the lung can be punctured.
(It is amazing how high in the neck the top portions of the lungs are
located.)

If the patient recovers well enough not to require cricothyrotomy,
just remove the needle or cannula and the wound will seal itself in short
order. Butterfly closures should prove adequate to approximate the
wound.

RAPID HEART RATE — A very rapid rate of 140 to 220 beats
per minute may be encountered suddenly and without warning in very
healthy individuals. This PAT (paroxysmal atrial tachycardia) has as
its first symptom, frequently, a feeling of profound weakness. The
victim generally stops what he is doing and feels better sitting down.
These attacks are self-limited, but they can be aborted by one of several
maneuvers. Holding one's breath and bearing down very hard may stop
this arrhythmia; closing one's eyes and pressing very firmly on the
eyeballs may also work; inducing vomiting with a finger down the throat
also works at times. Feel for the carotid pulse in the neck and gently
press on the enlarged portion of this vessel, one side at a time — this
also can work. Frequently, however, the victim must just wait for the

attack to pass. this arrhythmia will sometimes come on after a spate of activity. No medication is generally required.

A rapid heart rate after trauma or other stress may signify impending shock. The underlying cause should be treated. This may require fluid replacement or pain medication. Temperature elevations cause an increase in heart rate of 10 beats per minute for each degree above normal.

HYPERVENTILATION SYNDROME — This feeling of panic which results in very rapid breathing, with shallow breaths, causes the victim to lose carbon dioxide from the bloodstream. The resulting respiratory alkalosis will cause a numb feeling around the mouth, in the extremities, and if the breathing pattern persists, it can even lead to violent spasms of the hands and feet. This is a form of hysteria, which while more common in women in their 30's, can also appear in teenagers and healthy young adults. It would be helpful for them to rebreathe their air from a stuff sack to increase the carbon dioxide level in their bloodstream. They need to be reassured and told to slow down the breathing. It is fine for them to draw long, deep breaths — it is the rapid breathing that blows off so much CO_2.

If necessary, from the Non-Rx Oral Medication Module give Mobigesic 2 tablets or from the Rx Oral/Topical Medication Module you may give Atarax 25mg, 2 tablets. The Rx Injectable Module medication Vistaril 50 mg IM is helpful in treating hyperventilation. These drugs are being used in this instance as anti-anxiety drugs. This symptom in a diabetic is very dangerous, but can be prevented by proper diabetic management. High altitude stress can result in hyperventilation (see page 59.)

HICCUPS — These can be started by a variety of causes and are generally self-limited. Persistent hiccups can be a medically important symptom requiring professional evaluation and help in control. Several approaches to their control in camp may be tried — have the victim hold his breath for as long as possible or rebreathe air from a stuff sack — these maneuvers raise the carbon dioxide level and help stop the hiccup reflex mechanism. Drinking 5 to 6 ounces of ice water fast sometimes works; one may also close his eyes and press firmly on the eyeballs to stimulate the vagal blockage of the hiccup.

If these maneuvers do not work, from the Non-Rx kit give Mobigesic 2 tablets or from the Rx Oral/Topical Medication Module you may give Atarax 25mg, 2 tablets. The Rx Injectable Module medication Vistaril 50 mg IM is also effective for this condition. These doses may be repeated every 4 hours. Let the patient rest and try to avoid bothering him until bedtime. If still symptomatic at that point, have him re-breathe the air from inside his sleeping bag, to raise the carbon dioxide level in his blood stream, and if nothing else to muffle the sounds.

PNEUMONIA — BRONCHITIS — Infection of the airways in the lung (bronchitis) and its extension into the air sacks of the lung (pneumonia) will cause very high fever, persistent cough — frequently producing phlegm stained with blood, and cause prostration of the victim. From the non-Rx kit treat the fever with the Mobigesic and the cough with Benadryl 25 mg every 4 hours (see page 7). If you have the Rx Oral/Topical Unit you may treat sharp pleuritic chest pain with Tylenol #3. It is also a strong cough suppressor as mentioned on page 12. Cool with a wet cloth over the forehead as needed. Do not bundle the patient with a very high fever as this will drive the temperature only higher. The shivering cold feeling that the patient has is only proof that his thermal control mechanism is out of adjustment — trust the thermometer or the back of your hand to follow the patient's temperature. Encourage the patient to drink fluids, as fever and coughing lead to dehydration. This causes the bronchioles to fill with tenacious mucous. Force fluid if necessary to prevent this sputum from plugging up sections of the lung.

Provide antibiotic, from the Rx kit, either the Bactrim DS, 1 tablet twice daily or the doxycycline 100 mg twice daily until the fever has broken and then for an additional 4 days. Or, from the Rx Injectable Module you may give Rocephin 1 gm once daily, or 500 mg twice daily. Prepare a sheltered camp for the victim as best as circumstances permit.

PNEUMOTHORAX — Even in very healthy young adults and teenagers, it is possible for a bleb on the lung to break — for no apparent reason — and fill a portion of the chest cavity with air, thus collapsing part of one lung. A minor pneumothorax will also spontaneously take care of itself, with the air being reabsorbed and the lung re-expanding over 3 to 5 days. The classic sign of decreased breath sounds over the area of the collapse will be very difficult for the untrained observer, even with a stethoscope. But listen first to one side of the chest and then the other to see if there is a difference. Part of the difficulty lies in the fact that patients with chest pain do not breath deeply and all breath sounds are decreased. Other parts of the physical exam are even more subtle. In unexplained severe chest pain in an otherwise healthy individual, at normal altitude, this might be the cause.

Severe pneumothorax will have to be treated by a physician with removal of the trapped air with a large syringe, flutter valve, or by other methods currently employed in a hospital setting. If pain is severe and breathing difficult, the only choice is evacuation of the victim.

From the non-Rx Oral Medication Module you may give 2 Mobigesic for pain every 4 hours. If you have the Rx Oral/Topical Medication Module, give 1 or 2 Tylenol #3 every 4 hours. This can be augmented with Atarax 25 mg every 6 hours. Injectable pain medication is sometimes necessary to control this very severe pain. From the Rx Injectable Module you may give Nubain 10 mg every 4 hours as required.

LIGHTNING — Cardiopulmonary arrest is the most significant lightning injury. People screaming from fright or burns after an electrical bolt has struck are already out of immediate danger. Their wounds may be dressed later. Those who appear dead must have immediate attention as they may be salvaged. Generally, when dealing with mass casualities the wounded are cared for preferentially, while the dead are left alone. Not in this instance! The victim is highly unlikely to die unless cardiopulmonary arrest happens. Without CPR, nearly 75% of those suffering arrest die. As the heart tends to restart itself due to its inherent automaticity, the heart beat may return spontaneously in a short time. The respiratory system, however, may be shut down for 5 to 6 hours before being able to resume its normal rhythm. The lack of oxygen this would cause will allow a person whose heart has started spontaneously to die. While CPR is being performed, check for the pulse periodically. When the heart restarts, then maintain ventilations for the patient until respirations also resume. Attempt to continue this as long as possible, for even after many hours the victim may revive with no neurological defects, but only if CPR or respiration ventilation has been properly performed. *Remember*, after a lightning strike the victim's eyes may be fixed and dilated, respirations ceased, heart stopped, blood pressure 0/0 — all signs of clinical death. Pay no attention to these findings, but administer CPR as long as physically possible.

Lightning frequently causes vascular spasms in its victim. This can result in faint, or even nonpalpable pulses. When the vasospasm clears, which it generally does within a few hours, the pulses return.

Neurological defects are the second major consequence of lightning hits. Approximately 72% of victims suffer loss of consciousness and three-quarters of these people will have a cardiopulmonary arrest. Direct damage to the brain can result, but frequently the neurological defects, to include seizure activity and abnormal brain wave studies, eventually revert to normal. Two thirds of victims will have neurological defects of the lower half of their bodies, one-third paralysis of the upper half. Amnesia and confusion of events taking place after the accident are common, but usually transient.

Most will have amnesia, confusion, and short term memory loss that may last two to five days after the injury. These effects are similar to the electroconvulsive shock therapy used for certain psychiatric problems. The person may be able to talk intelligently, but shortly thereafter not remember the conversation had taken place — or even remember that they had ever seen the people they have talked to.

Burns from the lightning itself are generally not severe. Very high voltage is carried over the surface of conductors. The high voltage of lightning is similarly carried over the surface of the body with minimal internal burn damage, the so called "flashover effect."

Direct electrical burn damage can occur however, and when it does it usually consists of one of several types. *Linear* burns start at the head, progress down the chest, and split to continue down both legs. These burns are usually 1/2 to 1 1/2 inches in width and are first and second degree. They follow areas of heavy sweat concentration. *Punctate* burns appear like a buck shot wound. These are full thickness third degree burns that are discrete, round wounds, measuring from a few millimeters to a centimeter in width. These seldom require grafting as the area is so small. *Feathering*, or *ferning* burns are diagnostic of lightning injury. They fade within a few hours to days and require no treatment. This phenomena is not a true burn, but the effect of electron showers on the skin. They have a characteristic reddish fern appearance that covers the skin surface — particularly notable on the trunk. *Thermal* burns are from vaporization of surface moisture, combustion of clothing, heated metal buckles, etc. Thermal burns are the most common type of lightning associated burn and they can be first, second, or third degree.

The flashover effect saves most victims from burn trauma. However, as noted, burns do occur. Persons with head burns are two and a half times more likely to die than those without. Possibly more surprising, persons with leg burns are five times more likely to die than those who do not have them. This is most likely related to a ground current phenomenon.

The four mechanisms of direct lightning injury are: 1) direct strike, 2) splash, 3) step current, 4) blunt trauma. To minimize the chance of lightning injury, the following should be noted about these mechanisms:

1. *Direct strikes* are most likely when in the open, especially if carrying metal or objects above shoulder level. Shelter should be taken within the cone of safety described as a 45 degree angle down from a tall object, such as a tree or cliff face.
2. *Splash* injuries are perhaps the most common mechanism of lightning hit — the current striking a tree or other object, may jump to a person whose body has less resistance than

the object the lightning initially contacted. Splash injuries may occur from person to person, when several people are standing close together. It has jumped from fences after having struck the fence some distance away. It has splashed to people from plumbing fixtures inside houses that were struck. Avoid close proximity to walls, fences, plumbing, or other items that could be struck.

3. *Step current* is also called stride voltage and ground current. The lightning current spreads out in a wave along the ground from the struck object, with the current strength decreasing as the radius from the strike increases. If the victim's feet are at different distances from the point of the strike, and the resistance in the ground greater than through his body, he will complete a circuit. Large groups of people can be injured simultaneously in this manner. Keeping feet and legs together, while squatting down, minimizes the chances of step voltage injury.

4. *Blunt trauma*, or the sledgehammer effect, results from the force of the lightning strike, or the explosive shock wave which it produces. It may occur with the victim being force-ably knocked to the ground. Over 50% of victims will have their ear drums ruptured in one or both ears. This may result from direct thermal damage, the thunder shock wave, or even skull fractures from the blunt trauma. Barotrauma to the ears may be reduced by keeping the mouth open during times of great danger.

The above scenario has a person squatting with legs together and mouth open in a zone of safety, but not too near the nearby protective tree or cliff face. Spread party members out to maximize the chance that there will be survivors, and thus rescuers, if lightning strikes appear imminent. Get boats into a zone of safety near shore against the tree line or cliff face. Other than the immediate presence of lightning is there any warning? At times there will be the smell of ozone, hair may stand on end, and St. Elmo's fire may be present. Good luck!

HIGH ALTITUDE ILLNESS — The high altitude related illnesses can generally be avoided by gradual exposure to higher elevation, with the ascent rate not exceeding 1,000 feet per day when above 6,000 feet. The three major clinical manifestations of this disease complex are outlined below:

ACUTE MOUNTAIN SICKNESS (AMS) — Rarely encountered

below 6,500 feet (2,000 meters), it is common in persons going above 10,000 feet (3,000 meters) without taking the time to acclimatize for altitude. Symptoms beginning soon after ascent consist of headache (often severe), nausea, vomiting, shortness of breath, weakness, sleep disturbance and occasionally a periodic breathing known to physicians as Cheyne-Stokes breathing.

Prevention, as with all of the high altitude illness problems, is gradual ascent to an altitude above 9,000 feet and light physical activity for the first several days. For persons especially prone to AMS, it may be helpful to take acetazolamide (Diamox) 250 mg every 12 hours starting the day before ascent and continuing the next 3 to 5 days. This prescription drug should be added to your medical kit if you expect to encounter elevations above 9,000 feet. See further discussion of Diamox on page 13. Anecdotal stories have indicated the non-Rx medication Benadryl when taken 25 mg 4 times daily starting a day before ascent and continuing for first 5 days during the portion of the trip above 6,500 feet might help prevent symptoms of AMS — but this substance has not been adequately studied.

Treatment is descent and relief can often be felt even if the descent is only 2,000 to 3,000 feet (600 to 900 meters). Full relief can be obtained by descending to below 6,500 feet (2,000 meters). Stricken individuals should avoid heavy exercise, but sleep does not help as the breathing is slower during sleep and oxygen deprivation is worse. Oxygen will only help if taken continuously for 12 to 48 hours. Aspirin may be used for headache. Mobigesic from the non-Rx kit may be used. In addition to descent, Decadron (dexamethasone) 4 mg tablets every 6 hours until well below the altitude at which symptoms appeared has been shown to help treat AMS.[1] Decadron tablets or injection should be added to your medical kit if you expect to encounter elevations above 9,000 feet. See further discussion of decadron on pages 13 and 14.

HIGH ALTITUDE PULMONARY EDEMA (HAPE) — This problem is rare below 8,000 feet (2,50 meters), but occurs at higher altitude in those poorly acclimatized. It is more prone to occur in persons between the ages of 5 and 18 (the incidence is apparently less than .4% in persons over 21 and as high as 6% in those younger); in persons who have had this problem before; and in persons who have been altitude acclimatized and who are returning to high altitude after spending 2 or more weeks at sea level.

Symptoms develop slowly within 24 to 60 hours of arrival at high altitude with shortness of breath, irritating cough, weakness, rapid heart rate and headache which rapidly progress to intractable cough with

[1]Ferreira and Grundy, *Dexamethasone in the Treatment of Acute Mountain Sickness*, NEJM, Vol 312, No 21, page 1390, 23 May 1985.

bloody sputum, low-grade fever and increasing chest congestion. Symptoms may progress at night. Climbers should be evaluated by listening to their chests for a fine crackling sound (called rales) and by checking their resting pulse rate nightly. A pulse rate of greater than 110 per minute or respirations greater than 16 per minute after a 20 minute rest is an early sign of HAPE. Respirations over 20 per minute and pulse over 120 per minute indicate a medical emergency and the patient must be evacuated immediately. Without treatment, death usually occurs within 6 to 12 hours after onset of coma.

Descent to lower altitude is essential and should not be delayed. Oxygen may be of value if given continuously over the next 12 to 48 hours, starting at 6 liters/minute for the first 15 minutes, then reduced to 2 liters/minute. A snug face mask is better than nasal prongs. Oxygen may provide rapid relief in mild cases, however it should be continued for a minimum of 6 to 12 hours, if possible. Oxygen is not a substitute for descent in severe cases. A descent of as little as 2,000 to 3,000 feet (600 to 900 meters) may result in prompt improvement. Morphine sulfate, 15 mg by intramuscular injection may be of value, but should be given in extreme cases only. Diuretics have not proven to be of value. A recent anecdotal report indicated Procardia 20 mg sublingual followed by 20 mg capsule resulted in relief of symptoms within 10 to 15 minutes. The sublingual preparation is not available in the United States. Descent was also used in this patient's management. A repeat dose of sublingual and oral capsule was required the following night.[1]

CEREBRAL EDEMA (CE) — This is a less common event than AMS or HAPE just mentioned, but it is more dangerous. Death has occurred from CE at altitude as low as 8,000 feet (2,500 meters), but CE is rare below 11,500 feet (3,500 meters). The symptoms are increasingly severe headache, mental confusion, emotional behavior, hallucinations, unstable gait, loss of vision, loss of dexterity, and facial muscle paralysis. The victim may fall into a restless sleep, followed by a deep coma and death.

Descent is essential. Oxygen should be administered. Decadron (dexamethasone) should be given in large doses, namely 10 mg intravenously, followed by 4 mg every 6 hours intramuscularly until the symptoms subside. Response is usually noted within 12 to 24 hours and the dosage may be reduced after 2 to 4 days and gradually discontinued over a period of 5 to 7 days. Immediate descent and oxygen are recommended to prevent permanent neurological damage or death.

As can be noted from the above discussions of AMS, HAPE, and CE, the symptoms progress rather insidiously. They are not clear-cut,

[1]Oelz, Oswald, *A Case of High-Altitude Pulmonary Edema Treated With Nifedipine*, JAMA, Vol 257, No 6, page 780, 13 Feb 1987.

separate diseases — they often occur together. The essential therapy for each of them is recognition and descent. This is life saving and more valuable than the administration of oxygen or the drugs mentioned. To prevent them it is helpful to "climb high, but camp low" — ie, spend nights at the lowest camp elevation feasible.

OTHER HIGH ALTITUDE CONDITIONS — Generalized swelling of the face, arms, and legs can appear after arrival at high altitude and may persist for days or even weeks. It is more common in women than men. The cause is unknown and no treatment is required. The swelling disappears after descent. The use of diuretics to eliminate this problem should be discouraged as they can lead to increased problems with dehydration.

Hemorrhages of the retinal blood vessels (of the eye) can occur at altitude over 14,000 feet (4,300 meters) and is frequently found in climbers over 17,600 feet (5,365 meters). This condition rarely causes visual difficulty. There is no treatment. It resolves several weeks after return to sea level.

Increased flatulance may be noted in high altitude. Foods known to cause gas at lower altitude should be avoided. Simethicone products can be taken to help control this problem, such as Phazyme 125, 1 tablet with meals and at bed time. This medication is available without a prescription.

High Altitude Cachexia (HAC) is the name that has been given to the extreme weight loss that climbers note on long high altitude climbs, above 17,000 feet (5,200 meters). Providing adequate amounts of carbohydrate seems to curtail some muscle loss. Fats and proteins become less palatable at high altitude. Climbers need between 5,000 and 6,000 kcal/day — 55% from carbohydrates, 35% from fats, and 10% from proteins. Dehydration is a significant problem from respiratory loss in the cold, dry air and due to rapid breathing rates. Climbers become dehydrated, yet urinate a dilute urine, rather than concentrating and conserving body fluid as is usual under dehydration circumstances. Vitamin intake should be approximately 3 times the recommended daily allowances due to the high calorie intake. To consume 6,000 kcal/day, a person would have to be in excellent physical shape. Most healthy young people cannot use more than 4,200 kcal/day.

HYPOTHERMIA — The term "hypothermia" refers to the lowering of the body's core temperature to 95 degrees F; "profound hypothermia" is a core temperature lower than 90 degrees F. Another important point is that the term "hypothermia" applies to two distinctly different diseases. One is "chronic hypothermia," the slow onset hypothermia of the outdoors traveler exposed to conditions too cold for their equipment to adequately protect them; the other is "acute," or "immersion hypothermia," the rapid onset hypothermia of a person immersed in cold water.

These diseases are dissimilar in that the body's response to both is quite different. Ideal treatment is also quite different in the hospital setting; but in the field we sometimes must rely on the old fashion cuddle technique for both types of victims.[1]

Chronic Hypothermia — The essential ingredients in surviving this situation are: being prepared to prevent it, recognizing it if it occurs, and knowing how to treat it. Dampness and wind are the most devastating factors to be considered. Dampness as it can reduce the insulation of clothing and cause evaporative heat loss. Wind as the increased convection heat loss can readily strip away body energy, the so called "wind chill" effect. It is possible to die of hypothermia in temperatures far above freezing. Most hypothermia deaths occur in the 30 degree to 50 degree range.

Factors important to preventing hypothermia are a high level of pre-trip physical conditioning, adequate nutritional and hydration status of trip members, avoiding exhaustion, and availability of adequate insulation. There is increased risk of hypothermia in case of injury, especially shock, or if the above preventative conditions are inadequate.

An initial response to cold is vasoconstriction, or the clamping down of surface blood vessels. This prevents heat from being conducted to the surface by the blood and effectively increases the mantle, or outer layer depth, thus providing an increased insulation layer. If a person becomes profoundly hypothermic, with a core temperature below 90 degrees F, they have concentrated their blood volume into a small inner core. The amount of dehydration in these persons can be profound, approaching 5.5 liters in a person below 90 degrees F — or equivalent to the entire circulatory volume. Of course this fluid loss comes from not only the vascular space, but also fluid from between the cells and within the cells as the body slowly adjusts to the continuing heat loss by shrinking the blood volume in the core and increasing the effective depth of the mantle layer. This causes problems with the re-warming process as a sudden re-warming can lead to "re-warming shock." Hos-

[1]Editors note: Readers are referred to Dr Forgey's book *Hypothermia: Death by Exposure*, 185 pages, ICS Books, 1985. This book contains the official State of Alaska pre- and post treatment protocols for acute and chronic hypothermia and Dr Forgey's discussions of field management, anecdotal stories, equipment and material evaluations, physiology of heat production and heat preservation, and the pathology of heat loss, all written for the concerned layman. Price is $9.95 from the publisher.

SIGNS AND SYMPTOMS OF HYPOTHERMIA

CORE TEMP	SIGNS AND SYMPTOMS
99° to 97°F (37° to 36°C)	Normal temperature range Shivering may begin
97°to 95°F (36° to 35°C)	Cold sensation, goose bumps, unable to perform complex tasks with hands, shivering can be mild to, severe, skin numb
95° to 93°F (35° to 34°C)	Shivering intense, muscle incoordination becomes apparent, movements slow and labored, stumbling pace, mild confusion, may appear alert, unable to walk 30 ft. line properly — BEST FIELD TEST FOR EARLY HYPOTHERMIA
93° to 90°F (34° to 32°C)	Violent shivering persists, difficulty speaking, sluggish thinking, amnesia starts to appear and may be retrograde, gross muscle movements sluggish, unable to use hands, stumbles frequently, difficulty speaking, signs of depression
90° to 86°F (32° to 30°C)	Shivering stops in chronic hypothermia, exposed skin blue or puffy, muscle coordination very poor with inability to walk, confusion, incoherent, irrational behavior, BUT MAY BE ABLE TO MAINTAIN POSTURE AND APPEARANCE OF PSYCHOLOGICAL CONTACT
86° to 82°F (30° to 27.7°C)	Muscles severely rigid, semiconscious, stupor, loss of psychological contact, pulse and respirations slow, pupils can dilate
82° to 78°F (27° to 25.5°C)	Unconsciousness, heart beat and respiration erratic, pulse and heart beat may be inapparent, muscle tendon reflexes cease
78° to 75°F (25° to 24°C	Pulmonary edema, failure of cardiac and respiratory centers, probable death, DEATH MAY OCCUR BEFORE THIS LEVEL
59°F (15.2°C)	Lowest recorded temperature of chronic hypothermia survivor, Japan, reported 1986
48.2°F (9°C	Lowest recorded temperature of induced hypothermia in surgical patient with survival, 1958

FIGURE 12. SIGNS AND SYMPTOMS OF HYPOTHERMIA

pital methods of re-warming must be coupled with tight metabolic control by adjusting blood factors such as clotting, electrolytes, blood sugar levels, etc. Loss of tight control can occur more easily if a person is re-warmed too rapidly.

Re-warming shock and loss of metabolic control is the cause of death, not the so-called "after-drop" phenomenon in chronic hypothermia. After-drop, or the further lowering of core temperature after re-warming has started, is a physical property of matter and can be demonstrated in dead pigs and watermelons as well as humans. It amounts to an equilibration of thermal mass as the remaining heat in the body slowly leaches into the colder mantle layer. The amount of after-drop that occurs is dependent upon the rate of cooling that was occurring prior to the re-warming process, not the method of re-warming!

The treatment of the chronic hypothermic victim is to prevent further loss of heat and this generally means providing shelter or more adequate clothing. The victim is exhausted and thus requires rest and food. They are dehydrated and require fluids. If the victim can stand, a roaring fire can provide adequate, controlled heat. Chronic hypothermia victims are exhausted and will not be able to exercise themselves to warmth. Exercise is a method of generating heat, as is shivering, but when energy stores are consumed, the exhaustion commences and significant hypothermia will begin unless further heat loss is stopped.

Deepening hypothermia will lead to a semi-comatose state and worse. This victim needs to be evacuated to help. Wrap to prevent further heat loss and transport. Chemical heat packs, etc., can be added to the wrap to help offset further heat loss, but care must be taken not to burn the victim. If evacuation is not feasible, heat will have to be added slowly to avoid re-warming shock. Huddling with two rescuers naked with the victim in an adequate sleeping bag may be the only alternative. On all of my expeditions into northern Canada in the winter, we always carry a set of semi-rectangular bags that can twin so that such a rescue is feasible.

Acute Hypothermia — Afterdrop is, however, a problem in the "acute" or "immersion hypothermic" who has had a significant exposure to cold water. If the sum of air temperature and water temperature is less than 100, atmospheric conditions favor acute hypothermia if immersion were to occur. As a rule of thumb, a person who has been in water of 50 degrees or less for a period of 20 minutes or longer, is suffering from a severe amount of heat loss. That individual's thermal mass has been so reduced that they are in potentially serious condition. They should not be allowed to move around as this will increase the blood flow to their very cold skin and facilitate a profound circulatory induced after-drop; one that is so great as to be potentially lethal. If this same person is simply wrapped as a litter case and not provided outside heat, there is a real danger of them cooling below a lethal level due to this profound amount of heat loss. The ideal treatment is rapid re-warming of the acute hypothermic by placing them in hot water (110 degrees F) to allow rapid replacement of heat. These people may have an almost normal core temperature initially, but one that is destined to drop dramatically as their body equilibrates their heat store from their core to their very cold mantle. A roaring fire can be a life saver. If not available, huddling two naked rescuers with the victim in a large sleeping bag may be the only answer — the same therapy that might have to be employed in the field treatment of chronic hypothermia under some conditions.

Cold water submersion[1] — is always associated with asphyxiation and simultaneous hypothermia. The asphyxiation results in brain death so that prompt rescue and immediate implementation of CPR play an important role in the survival of the victim. Total submersion in cold water results in rapid core cooling which results in a lower oxygen demand by the brain and other body tissues and increases the chance of survival over that of a victim of warm water submersion. Full recovery after 10 to 40 minutes of submersion can occur. CPR must be continued until the body has been warmed to at least 86 degrees F. If still unresponsive at that temperature, they may be considered dead. It may take several hours of CPR while the victim is being properly re-warmed to make this determination. The hospital management of victims of cold water submersion is very complex. These victims are best transferred to centers experienced with this problem, but the victim will never have a chance if rescuers do not implement CPR immediately.

FROST NIP — Frost nip, or light frostbite, can be readily treated in the field if recognized early enough. When detected, you should cup your hands and blow upon the affected parts to effect total rewarming. Under identical exposure conditions, some people are more prone to this than others. On one of my trips into subarctic Canada, one of my companions almost constantly frost-nipped his nose at rather mild temperatures (-20°F.) We frequently had to warn him, as he seemed oblivious to the fact that the tip of his nose would repeatedly frost.

---

[1]There is a distinct difference between immersion and submersion. Submersion indicates that the victim is entirely under water; immersion means that the head is above water.

FROSTBITE — Frostbite represents freezing of skin tissue. Traditionally, several degrees of frostbite are recognized, but the treatment for all is the same and the actual degree of severity will not be known until after the patient has been treated and the amount of damage then (readily) identified.

For victims with deep frostbite, rapid warming is the most effective treatment. Refreezing would result in substantial tissue loss. The frozen part should not be thawed if there is any possibility of refreezing the part. Also, once the victim has been thawed, very careful management of the thawed part is required. The patient actually becomes a stretcher case if the foot is involved. For that reason, it may be necessary to leave the foot or leg(s) frozen and allow the victim to walk back to the evacuation point or facility where the thawing will take place. Peter Freuchen, the great Greenland explorer, once walked days and miles keeping one leg frozen, knowing that when the leg thawed, he would be helpless. He lost his leg, but saved his life!

When superficial frostbite is suspected, thaw immediately so that it does not become a more serious, deep frostbite. Warm the hands by withdrawing them into the parka through the sleeves — avoid opening the front of the parka to minimize heat loss. Feet should be thawed against a companion or cupped in your own hands in a roomy sleeping bag, or otherwise in an insulated environment.

The specific therapy for a deep frozen extremity is rapid thawing in warm water (approx. 110°F.). This thawing may take 20 to 30 minutes, but it should be continued until all paleness of the tops of the fingers or toes has turned to pink or burgundy red, but no longer. This will be very painful and will require pain medication (Rx Tylenol #3, 2 tablets at the start of the procedure, or 10 mg of Nubain IM).

Avoid opening the blisters that form. Do not cut skin away, but allow the digits to autoamputate over the next *3 months*. Blisters will usually last 2 to 3 weeks — these must be treated with care to prevent infections (best done in a hospital with gloved attendants).

A black carapace will form in severe frostbite. This is actually a form of dry gangrene. This carapace will gradually fall off with amazingly good healing beneath — efforts to hasten the carapace removal generally result in infection, delay in healing and increased loss of tissue. Leave these blackened areas alone. The black carapace separation can take over six months, but it is worth the wait. Without surgical interference, most frostbite wounds heal in six months to a year. All persons heading into the bush should already have had their tetanus booster (within the previous 10 years). Treat for shock routinely with elevation of feet and lowering of head, as this will frequently occur when these people enter a warm environment.

If a frozen member has thawed and the patient must be transported, use cotton between toes (or fluff sterile gauze from the emergency kit and place between toes) and cover other areas with a loose bandage to protect the skin during sleeping bag stretcher evacuation. The use of Spenco 2nd skin for blister care would be ideal — see page 43. If a fracture also exists, immobilize when in the field, loosely so as not to impair the circulation any further.

FROZEN LUNG — or pulmonary chilling, more properly, as no tissue is actually frozen, occurs when breathing rapidly at very low temperatures, generally below -20°F. There is burning pain, sometimes coughing of blood, frequently asthmatic wheezing and, with irritation of the diaphragm, pain in the shoulder(s) and upper stomach that may last for 1 to 2 weeks. The treatment is bed rest, steam inhalations, drinking extra water, humidification of quarters and no smoking. Avoid by using parka hoods, face masks or breathing through mufflers which allow the rebreathing of warmed, humidified, expired air.

IMMERSION FOOT — This results from wet, cool conditions with temperature exposures from 68°F. (20°C) down to freezing. There are two stages of this problem: the first stage, in which the foot is cold, swollen, waxy, mottled with dark burgundy to blue splotches. This foot is resilient to palpation, whereas the frozen foot is very hard. Skin is sodden and friable. Loss of feeling makes walking difficult. The second stage lasts from days to weeks. The feet are swollen, red and hot; blisters form; infection and gangrene are common.

To prevent this problem, avoid non-breathing (rubber) footwear when possible, dry the feet and change wool socks when feet get wet or sweaty (every 3 to 4 hours, if necessary), periodically elevate, air, dry, massage the feet to promote circulation. Avoid tight, constricting clothing.

Treatment differs from frostbite and hypothermia in the following ways: 1) Give the patient 10 grains of aspirin every 6 hours to help decrease platelet adhesion and clotting ability of the blood, 2) Give additional Tylenol #3 every 4 hours for pain, but discontinue as soon as possible, 3) Provide an ounce of hard liquor (30 ml) every hour while awake and 2 ounces (60 ml) every 2 hours during sleeping hours — to vasodilate or increase the flow of blood to the feet. If you are unsure whether or not you are dealing with immersion foot or frostbite, or if you may have suffered both, treat as for frostbite.

CHILBLAINS — This results from exposure of dry skin to temperatures from low 60°F to freezing. The skin is red, swollen, frequently tender and itching. This is the mildest form of cold injury, no tissue loss results. Treatment is the prevention of further exposure with protective clothing over bare skin and the use of ointments if available, such as A & D Ointment or Vaseline (white petrolatum). The hydrocortisone .5% cream from the non-Rx kit will help when applied 4 times daily.

HEAT STRESS — High environmental temperatures are frequently aggravated by the amount of work being done, the humidity, reflection of heat from rock, sand or other structures (even snow!) and the lack of air movement. It takes a human approximately 5 to 7 days to become heat acclimated. Once heat stress adaptation takes place, there will be a decrease in the loss of salt in the sweat produced, thus conserving electrolytes. Another major change that occurs is the rapid formation of sweat and the formation of larger quantities of sweat. Thus, the body is able to start its response to an elevation in the core temperature more rapidly and to utilize its efficient cooling mechanism, sweating, more fully and with less electrolyte disturbance to the body.

Salt (NaCl) lost in sweat during work can normally be replaced at mealtime. An unacclimatized man working an 8 hour shift would sweat 4 to 6 liters of sweat. The salt content is high, namely 3 to 5 gram/liter of sweat. With acclimatization the salt concentration drops (1 to 2 gram/liter of sweat). Thus an acclimatized man might lose 6 to 16 grams of salt during an 8 hour shift in 6 to 8 liters of sweat. The unacclimatized man could lose a total of 18 to 30 grams of salt in 4 to 6 liters of sweat. *The average American diet contains 10 to 15 grams/day of salt.* Thus, an unacclimatized worked could be in a 3 to 20 gram salt deficit per day. In the 7 to 10 days that it would take his body to become conditioned to heat stress, the total salt deficit could become substantial.

A worry in discussing heat illness prevention with the general public is the over-riding requirement that a heat stressed individual obtain adequate fluid replacement. If the public focuses on salt replacement, to the exclusion of adequate water intake, the individual may become salt loaded and accelerate his dehydration. Generally, however, an excess of salt or water over actual needs is readily controlled by kidney excretion.

Depletion of body salt *can* lead to progressive dehydration because the body will attempt to maintain a balance between electrolyte concentration in tissue fluids with that in the cells. Deficient salt intake with continued intake of water tends to dilute tissue fluid, which suppresses antidiuretic hormone (ADH) of the pituitary gland, which prevents the kidney from reabsorbing water. The kidney will then excrete a dilute urine containing little salt. This will preserve the low salt content of the body, but it will add to body water loss considerably. The electrolyte concentration of body fluids will be maintained, but at the cost of depleting body water with resulting dehydration. Under heat stress, this can result in symptoms of heat exhaustion similar to those resulting from water restriction, but with more severe signs of circulatory insufficiency and notably little thirst. Absence of chloride in the urine (less than 3gm/liter) is diagnostic of salt deficiency.

The ideal replacement fluid for the unacclimatized worker would be lightly salted water (0.1% or 1 tsp/gal), to prevent water or salt depletion. They will need 13 to 20 ounces of water before the activity and 3 to 6 ounces of water every 10 to 15 minutes during the active period. Water should not be withheld longer than 30 minute intervals. Replacement fluids should not contain greater sugar concentrations than 2.5 grams per 100 ml of water, or gastric emptying will be slowed. Acclimatized subjects will need only water as a replacement fluid, but will need 1 liter (32) ounces per hour. Thirst may lag behind requirements, so that oral replacement should be voluntarily done before thirst even becomes noticeable. Water deprivation is dangerous and should be avoided.

With no water available, how long could a person expect to survive? The answer is generally dependent upon the temperature and the amount of activity. At a temperature of 120°F with no water available, the victim would expect to survive about 2 days (regardless of activity). This temperature is so high that survival would not be increased beyond 2 days by even 4 quarts of water. Ten quarts might provide an extra day. At 90°F with no water, the person could survive about 5 days if he walked during the day, 7 days if travel was only at night or if no travel was undertaken at all. With 4 quarts of water, survival would extend to 6 1/2 days for day travel and to 10 days for night travel. With 10 quarts, days of survival would increase to 8 and 15 respectively. If the highest temperature was 60°F, with no water, the active person could expect to survive 8 days, the inactive person 10 days.

HEAT CRAMPS — Salt depletion can result in nausea, twitching of muscle groups and at times severe cramping of abdominal muscles, legs, or elsewhere.

Treatment consists of stretching the muscles involved (avoid aggressive massage), resting in a cool environment, and replacing salt losses. Generally 10 to 15 grams of salt and generous water replacement should be adequate treatment.

HEAT EXHAUSTION — This is a classic example of SHOCK, but in this case encountered while working in a hot environment. The body has dilated the blood vessels in the skin, hoping to divert heat from the core to the surface for cooling. However, this dilation is so pronounced, coupled with the profuse sweating and loss of fluid — also a part of the cooling process, that the blood pressure to the entire system falls too low to adequately supply the brain and the visceral organs. The patient will have a rapid heart rate, and will have the other findings associated with shock: Pale color, nausea, dizziness, headache, and a light-headed feeling. Generally the patient is sweating profusely, but this may not be the case. The temperature is as usual in shock, namely it may be low, normal, or mildly elevated.

Treat as for shock. Have the patient lie down immediately, elevate the feet to increase the blood supply to the head, cover if body temperature is cool or the skin clammy. Also, provide copious water; 10 to 15 grams of salt would also be helpful, but water is the most important, minimum of 1 to 2 quarts. Obviously, fluids can only be administered if the patient is conscious. If unconscious, elevate the feet 3 feet above head level, protect from aspiration of vomit, try to revive with an ammonia inhalant. Then give water when the patient awakens.

HEAT STROKE (SUN STROKE) — This represents the complete breakdown of the heat control process (thermal regulation) in the human body. There is a total loss of the ability to sweat, core temperatures rise over 105°F *rapidly* and will soon exceed 115°F and result in death if this is not treated aggressively. THIS IS A TRUE EMERGENCY. The patient will be confused and rapidly become unconscious. Immediately move into shade or erect a hasty barrier for shade. If possible employ immediate immersion in ice water to lower the temperature. Once the core temperature lowers to 102°F the victim is removed and the temperature carefully monitored. It may continue to fall or suddenly raise again.

Further cooling with wet cloths may suffice. IV solutions of normal saline are started in the clinic setting — in the wilderness, douse the victim with the coolest water possible. Massage limbs to allow the cooler blood of the extremities to return to core circulation more readily. Sacrifice your water supply — if necessary, urinate on the victim, fan and massage to provide the best coolant effect possible. This person should be evacuated as soon as possible, for his thermal regulation mechanism is quite literally unstable and will be labile for an undeterminable length of time. He should be placed under a physician's care as soon as possible. Terminate the expedition, if necessary, to evacuate.

PRICKLY HEAT — This is a heat rash caused by the entrapment of sweat in glands in the skin. This can result in irritation and frequently severe itching. Treatment includes cooling and drying the involved area and avoiding conditions that may induce sweating for awhile. Topical medications are less effective than the steps just mentioned, but a good topical would be any of the corticosteroid lotions or creams (an example would be cordran lotion or cream). This cream could be applied three times a day during the symptomatic period. From the Rx kit, apply a light coat of the Topicort ointment every 12 hours or from the non-Rx kit apply Hydrocortisone cream .5% every 6 hours.

ABDOMINAL PAIN — Even with years of clinical experience and unlimited laboratory and x-ray facilities, abdominal pain can be a diagnostic dilemma.For the wilderness traveler confronted with abdominal pain, the major decision is concerning the seriousness of the problem — should the trip be terminated or evacuation started, or can it be waited out or safely treated in the bush. For some travelers in isolation where there is no chance of rescue, a sensible treatment protocol must be activated.

Any abdominal pain that lasts longer than 1 hour is cause for serious concern — seek help if possible.

TABLE 3
Symptoms and Signs of Abdominal Pathology

	Burning	Nausea	Food Related	Diarrhea	Fever
Gastritis/ulcer	xx	x	xx		
Pancreatitis	xx	x	x		x
Hiatal Hernia	xx		x		
Gall Bladder		xx	xx		x
Appendicitis		x			x
Gastro-enteritis		xx		xx	x
Diverticulitis			xx	x	
Hepatitis		xx	x		x
Food Poisoning		xx	xx	xx	x

xx   A frequent or intense symptom
x   Common, less intense symptom
Blank   Less likely to produce this symptom

Diagnosis is frequently derived by the type of pain, location, cause, fever — all from the history — as well as certain aspects of the physical exam and the clinical course that develops.

Burning — upper part of the stomach in the middle (mid- epigastrium) is probably **GASTRITIS**. If allowed to persist this can develop into an

ULCER — which is a crater eaten into the stomach wall. Severe persistent mid-epigastric pain, that is frequently burning in nature, can be **PANCREATITIS**. This is a serious problem, but rare. Alcohol consumption can cause pancreatitis, as well as gastritis and ulcer formation; it must be avoided if pain in this area develops. Reflux of stomach acid up the esophagus, sometimes caused by a **HIATAL HERNIA**, will cause the same symptoms. Treatment for all of the above is aggressive antacid therapy. These conditions can be made worse with spicy food, tomato products, and other foods high in acid content and these should be avoided. Avoid any medication that contains aspirin, such as the Mobigesic recommended for the non-Rx kit, but Tylenol #3 can be given for pain. Acid suppression medication such as Tagamet, Zantac, or Pepcid can help greatly, but these medications can make the user more vulnerable to traveler's diarrhea and other infectious disease from which normal or high stomach acid would otherwise help provide protection. A safer medication for persons afflicted with frequent heart burn not responsive to antacids would be Carafate taken 1 gram 4 times daily. This prescription drug should be added to the wilderness medical kit if necessary.

Nausea with pain in the patient's right upper quadrant may be from a **GALL BLADDER** problem. This discomfort is made worse with eating — sometimes even smelling — fatty foods. While cream would initially help the pain of gastritis or ulcer, it would cause an immediate increase in symptoms if the gall bladder is involved. Treatment is avoidance of fatty foods. Nausea can be treated with the meclizine 25 mg tablets from the non-Rx kit, but would respond much better to the Atarax 25 mg given every 4 to 6 hours from the Rx Oral/Topical kit or Vistaril 25 mg IM from the Rx Injectable kit. Pain may be treated with 2 Mobigesic every 4 hours if it is likely that you are not dealing with a gastritis or ulcer. There is no burning sensation with gall bladder pain. A safe medication would be the use of Tylenol #3 or even the injectable Nubain 10 mg IM every 4 to 6 hours if available. The development of a fever is an important development which could indicate an infection in the blocked gall bladder. An infection of the gall bladder is a surgical emergency. This should be treated with the strongest antibiotic available. If the injectable Rx unit is carried, give Rocephin 1 gram IM, followed by 1 gram in 12 hours and then 1 gram every 24 hours. Lacking that give Doxycycline 100 mg every 12 hours from the oral Rx kit. Continue to treat the nausea and pain as indicated. Offer as much fluid as they can tolerate. Gall bladder disease is most common in overweight people in their 40's. It is more common in women.

The possibility of **APPENDICITIS** is a major concern as it can occur in any age group, and that includes healthy wilderness travelers. It is fortunately rare. While surgery is the treatment of choice, probably as many as 70% of people not treated with surgery can survive this disaster, even more with appropriate IV therapy. The classic presentation of this illness is a vague feeling of discomfort around the umbilicus (navel). Temperature may be low grade, 99.6 to 100.6 at first. Within a matter of hours the discomfort turns to pain and localizes in the right lower quadrant, most frequently on a point 2/3 of the way between the navel and the very top of the right pelvic bone (anterior-superior iliac spine). This pain syndrome can be elicited from the patient by asking two questions: Where did you first start hurting? (belly button); Now where do you hurt? (right lower quadrant as described). Those answers mean appendicitis until it is ruled out. It is possible but unusual to have diarrhea with appendicitis. Diarrhea generally means the patient does not have appendicitis.

Sometimes even full laboratory and x-ray facilities can do no better in evaluating this diagnosis — the ultimate answer will come from surgical exploration. If a surgeon has doubts, he might wait, with the patient safely in a hospital or at home under close supervision. But the patient with those symptoms should certainly be taken to a surgeon as soon as possible.

In the examination of the acute abdomen, several maneuvers can assess the seriousness of the situation. The first is the determination of guarding to palpation. If the patient has a rigid stomach to gentle pushing, this can mean that extreme tenderness and irritation of the peritoneum, or abdominal wall lining, exists. Use only gentle pushing. If there is an area of the abdomen where it does not hurt to push, apply pressure rather deeply. Suddenly take your hand away — if pain flares over the area of suspect tenderness, this is called "referred rebound tenderness" and it means that the irritation has reached an advanced stage. This person should be evacuated to surgical help at once.

What can you do if you are in the deep bush, say the Back River of Canada, without the faintest hope of evacuating the patient? Move the patient as little as possible. No further prodding of the abdomen should be done, as their only hope is that the appendix will form an abscess that will be walled-off by the bodily defense mechanisms. Give no food — provide small amounts of water, Gatorade, fruit drinks as tolerated. With advanced disease the intestines will stop working and the patient will vomit any excess. This will obviously cause a disturbance to the gut and possibly rupture the appendix or the abscess — however, there is not much that you can do about it.

Treat for pain, nausea, and with antibiotics as indicated in the paragraph above on Gall Bladder infection.

The abscess should form 24 to 72 hours following onset of the illness.

Many surgeons would elect to open and drain this abscess as soon as the patient is brought to their control. Other surgeons would feel that it is best to leave the patient alone at this time and allow the abscess to continue the walling-off process. These surgeons feel that there is so much inflammation present, surgery only complicates the situation further. Within 2 to 3 weeks the patient may be able to move with minimal discomfort.

One form of therapy never to be employed when there is a suspicion of appendicitis is the use of a laxative. The action of the laxative may cause disruption of the appendix abscess with resultant generalized peritonitis (massive abdominal infection).

It is currently thought that there is no justification for the prophylactic removal of an appendix in an individual, unless he is planning to move to a very remote area without medical help for an extended period of time and it is known from x-ray that he has a fecolith in the region of the appendix. Otherwise, the possible latter complications of surgical adhesions may well outweigh the "benefit" of such a procedure.

VOMITING — Nausea and vomiting are frequently caused by infections known as gastroenteritis. Many times these are viral so that antibiotics are of no value. These infections will usually resolve without treatment in 24 to 48 hours. Fever seldom is high, but may briefly be high in some cases. Fever should not persist above 100 degrees longer than 12 hours. Treatment may be with meclizine, Atarax, or Vistaril — as indicated in the discussions of those drugs — for symptomatic relief. Vomiting without diarrhea will not require the use of an antibiotic. If the vomiting is caused from severe illness, such as an ear infection, then use of antibiotic to treat the underlying cause is justified.

The nausea induced by high altitude is discussed on page 59.

Nausea is a frequent complaint of many viral illnesses. One of particular importance to wilderness travelers in under-developed countries is HEPATITIS caused by the Hepatitis A virus (formerly called infectious hepatitis.) This disease is common and worldwide. Its symptoms vary from a minor flu-like illness to fatal liver failure. It takes two to six weeks to develop the disease from time of contact. After 3 to 10 days of nausea, vomiting, lethargy and fever, the urine will turn dark, followed by a yellow color in the whites of the eyes and in severe cases, yellow skin. This jaundice reaches a peak in 1 to 2 weeks and gradually resolves during a 2 to 4 week recovery phase. Urine, blood and stool should be considered very contaminated — these must be carefully disposed of to prevent spread of the disease. Personal hygiene helps prevent this spread, but isolation of the patient is not strictly required. In most cases no specific treatment is required — after a few days appetite generally returns and bed confinement is no longer required. Restrictions of diet have no value.

The patient may safely return to full activity before the jaundice completely resolves — the best guideline is the disappearance of the lethargy and feeling of illness that appeared in the first stages of the disease. If profound prostration occurs, and certainly when feasible, the trip should be terminated for the patient and he should be placed under medical care. If possible, contacts should receive Gamma-globulin 0.02 ml/kg IM. The use of Gamma-globulin prophylactically is discussed under IMMUNIZATION (Appendix A).

MOTION SICKNESS — To prevent and treat motion sickness, a very useful non-Rx drug is meclizine 25 mg, taken 1 hour prior to departure for all day protection. There is minimal drowsiness and other side effects with this medication. Transderm Scope, a patch containing scopolamine, has been developed for prevention of motion sickness, but this requires an Rx. Each patch may be worn behind the ear for 3 days. It is fairly expensive, but very worth while if you are prone to this malady. There tends to be higher frequency of side effects with this medication in elderly people, such as visual problems, confusion, and loss of temperature regulation. A valuable drug to treat motion sickness is the Atarax 25 mg every 4 hours as needed from the Rx Oral/Topical kit, or the Vistaril 25 mg IM every 4 hours as needed from the Rx Injectable kit.

DIARRHEA — is the expulsion of watery stool. This malady is usually self limited, but can be a threat to life, depending upon its cause and extent. Diarrhea can be a symptom of diverticulitis, cholera, food or water contamination, parasites, colitis and other inflammations of the bowel, and rarely with appendicitis and gall bladder disease.

Diverticulitis is found in people over the age of 40 and is generally only a condition of the elderly. Diverticulae are little pouches that form on the large intestine, or colon, from a weakness that develops over time in the muscles of its wall. These are of no trouble unless they become infected. Infection causes diarrhea, fever, and painful cramping. Treatment is with antibiotic such as the Doxycycline 100 mg every 12 hours. Use Diasorb as described on page 7.

Colitis and other inflammations of the bowel cause repeated bouts of diarrhea. At times a fever may be present. These cases are chronic, and like diverticulitis, the diagnosis must be made with barium enema x-ray or colonoscopy. If in doubt, treat with Doxycycline 100 mg every 12 hours. These conditions require specific drugs for treatment, such as the steroids included with the Rx Oral/Topical and Injectable kits, but unless the person has a prior history of these diseases, their use in the wilderness is inappropriate.

Traveler's diarrhea is from infectious causes so that prevention seems an appropriate priority.

Prevention is effected by staying alert. Water sources must be known pure or treated as indicated on pages 79 and 82. Tainted food should be avoided. Once dehydrated or freeze-dried food has been reconstituted, it should be stored as carefully as any fresh, unprocessed food. Be wary of fresh fruits and vegetables in developing countries. Peel all such items, or thoroughly rinse with purified water, or boil for 10 minutes minimum. Often, in countries lacking refrigeration, fruits and vegetables are "freshened" on the way to market by sprinkling these items frequently with water from road side drainage ditches. The use of human fertilizer makes this water very contaminated. This contamination is not eliminated by drying or wiping with a cloth. Certain animal products are tainted in various parts of the world, particularly at specific times of the year. Know the flora and fauna which your expedition plans to utilize from local sources!

The definition of diarrhea is 2 to 3 times the number of bowel movements that are customary for an individual. These stools must be either soft, meaning that they will take the shape of a container, or watery, meaning that they can be poured. At least one associated symptom of fever, chills, abdominal cramps, nausea, or vomiting must be present. This will generally mean 4 unformed stools in a day, or 3 unformed stools in an 8 hours period when accompanied by at least one other symptom listed above. The disease is generally self limiting, lasting 2 to 3 days. As many as 75% of people will have abdominal pain and cramps, 50% will have nausea, and 25% will have vomiting and fever.

An acute onset of watery diarrhea usually means that an enterotoxigenic E. coli is the cause, but shigellosis will also first present in this manner. Symptoms of bloody diarrhea or mucoid stools are frequently seen with invasive pathogens such as Shigella, Campylobacter, or Salmonella. The presence of chronic diarrhea with malabsorption and gas indicates possible Giardia. Rotovirus disease starts with vomiting in 80% of cases.

In a study of U.S. students in Mexico, the cause of diarrhea was found to be: enterotoxigenic E. coli 40%; enteroadherent E. coli 5%; Giardia lamblia and Entamoeba histolytica 2%; Rotovirus 10%; Aeromonas 1%; Shigella 15%; Salmonella 7%; Campylobacter 3%; and unknown 17%.

Various medications have been shown effective in preventing traveler's diarrhea, but a recent consensus meeting of experts has discouraged their use due to cost, exposing people to drug side effects, possible development of resistant germs due to antibiotic overuse, and the normally benign course of the disease. Pepto-Bismol 2 ounces (4 tablespoons) or 2 tablets taken 4 times daily can prevent this problem. Ugh! There is about 8 aspirin tablets worth of salicylate in that quantity of Pepto-Bismol.

The other drug mentioned was an Rx antibiotic included in this kit. The doxycycline 100 mg once daily for prevention can be considered for short, important trips where even short bouts of diarrhea cannot be tolerated. An alternative course is simply to treat the problem if and when it occurs. This makes sense for long trips where taking daily antibiotic is less justified as mentioned above.

Treatment of traveler's diarrhea is Doxycycline 100 mg taken 1 tablet twice daily or Bactrim-DS 1 tablet twice daily. Treating with Pepto-Bismol requires 2 tablespoons every 30 minutes for 8 doses. An effective treatment is the Diasorb from the Non-Rx Oral Medication kit. See listing on page 7 for instructions on use. Tylenol #3 will stop diarrhea and cramping by taking 1 tablet every 4 to 6 hours. I would use the Diasorb and 1 of the above antibiotics as a first choice in treatment, adding the Tylenol #3 if symptoms persisted or cramping was very severe. Other Rx drugs commonly used in treating diarrhea are Lomotil (2 tablets every 6 hours) or Imodium (2 caps at the onset, then 1 after each loose stool).

Oral Fluid Replacement Therapy — Profound diarrheas from any source may cause severe dehydration and electrolyte imbalance. The non-vomiting patient must receive adequate fluid replacement, equaling his stool loss plus about 2 liters per day. The Center for Disease Control has recommended the following oral replacement cocktails to replace the losses of profound diarrhea:

Prepare two separate glasses of the following:

Glass 1) Orange, apple or other fruit juice
(rich in potassium) . . . . 8 ounces
Honey or corn syrup (glucose necessary
for absorption of essential salts) . . . . 1/2 teaspoon
Salt, table (rich in sodium and chloride) . . . 1 pinch

Glass 2) Water (carbonated or boiled) . . . . 8 ounces
Soda, baking (sodium bicarbonate) . . 1/4 teaspoon

Drink alternately from each glass. Supplement with carbonated beverages or water and tea made with boiled or carbonated water as desired. Avoid solid foods and milk until recovery.

It should be noted that the use of Gatorade, available in a powdered form from many backpacking specialty shops, may be used to replace Glass 1, except that the water used must be boiled or carbonated, as mentioned under Glass 2. It should also be diluted with twice the volume of fluid recommended by the manufacturer.

Throughout the world UNICEF and WHO distribute an electrolyte replacement product called Oralyte. It must be reconstituted with adequately purified water.

WATER PURIFICATION FOR DRINKING — Water can be purified adequately for drinking by mechanical, physical, and chemical means.

The clearest water possible should be chosen or attempts made to clarify the water prior to starting any disinfectant process. Water with high particulate count, with clay or organic debris, allows higher bacterial counts and tends to be more heavily contaminated. In preparing potable, or drinkable, water we are attempting to lower the germ counts to the point that the body can defend itself against the remaining numbers. We are not trying to produce sterile water, that would generally be impractical.

The use of chlorine based systems has been effectively used by municipal water supply systems for years. There are two forms of chlorine readily available to the outdoors traveler. One is liquid chlorine laundry bleach and the other is Halazone tablets. Laundry bleach that is 4 to 6 percent can make clear water safe to drink if 2 drops are added to 1 quart of water. This water must be mixed thoroughly and let stand for 30 minutes before drinking. This water should have a slight chlorine odor. If not, the original laundry bleach may have lost some of its strength and you should repeat the dose and let stand an additional 15 minutes prior to drinking.

Halazone tablets from Abbott Laboratories are also effective. They are actually quite stable with a shelf life of 5 years, even when exposed to temperatures over 100°F occasionally. Recent articles in outdoor literature have stated that Halazone has a short shelf life and that it loses 75% of its activity when exposed to air for two days. Abbott Labs refutes this and has proven the efficacy of use for Halazone sufficiently to receive FDA approval. A clue to their stability is that they turn yellow and have an objectionable odor when they decompose. Check for this before use. Five tablets should be added to a quart of clear water for adequate chlorination.

Chlorine based systems are very effective against virus and bacteria. They work best in neutral or slightly acid waters. As the active form of the chlorine, namely hypochlorous acid (HClO), readily reacts with nitrogen containing compounds such as ammonia, high levels of organic debris decrease its effectiveness. The amount of chlorine bleach or Halazone added must be increased if the water is alkaline or contaminated with organic debris.

Iodine is a very effective agent against protozoan contamination such as *Giardia lamblia* and *Entamoeba hystolytica* which tend to be resistant to chlorine. Further, iodine is not as reactive to ammonia or other organic debris by-products, thus working better in cloudy water. Tincture of iodine as found in the home medicine chest may be used as the source of the iodine. Using the commonly available 2% solution, 5 drops should be added to clear water or 10 drops to cloudy water, and the resultant mix should be allowed to stand 30 minutes prior to drinking.

The Armed Forces were responsible for developing a solid tablet that provided a source of iodine. Tetraglycine hydroperiodide is available as Globaline or Potable Aqua, or as Army surplus water purification tablets. An elemental iodine concentration of 3 to 5 ppm (parts per million) is necessary to kill amoeba and their cysts, algae, bacteria and their spores, and enterovirus. One tablet of Potable Aqua will provide 8 ppm iodine concentration per quart. If the water is clear a ten minute wait is required; for cloudy water wait 20 minutes before consuming. At near freezing temperatures, wait a full 30 minutes before drinking.

Crystals of iodine can also be used to prepare a saturated iodine-water solution for use in disinfecting drinking water. Four to eight grams of USP grade iodine crystals can be placed in a 1 ounce glass bottle. Water added to this bottle will dissolve an amount of iodine based upon its temperature. It is this saturated iodine-water solution which is then added to the quart of water. The amount added to produce a final concentration of 4 ppm will vary according to temperature as indicated in the chart:

TEMPERATURE	VOLUME	CAPFULLS
37°F (3°C)	20.0 cc	8
68°F (20°C)	13.0 cc	5+
77°F (25°C)	12.5 cc	5
104°F (40°C)	10.0 cc	4

*Assuming 2½ cc capacity for a standard 1 ounce glass bottle cap

This water should be stored for 15 minutes before drinking. If the water is turbid, or otherwise contaiminated, the amounts of saturated iodine solution indicated above should be doubled and the resultant water stored 20 minutes before using. This product is now commercially available as Polar Pure through many outdoor stores and catalog houses.

Mechanical filtration methods are also useful in preparing drinking water. They normally consist of a screen with sizes down to 6 microns in size which are useful in removing tapeworm eggs (25 microns) or Giardia lamblia (7 to 15 microns). These screens inclose an activated charcoal filter element which removes many disagreeable tastes. As most bacteria have a diameter smaller than 1 micron, bacteria and the even smaller viral species are not removed by filtration using these units. For water to be safe after using one of these devices it must be pre-treated with chlorine or iodine exactly as indicated above prior to passage through the device. While these filters remove clay and organic debris, they will plug easily if the water is very turbid. A concern with the charcoal filter usage is the possibility for them to become contaminated with bacteria while being used and possibly allowing considerable passage of bacteria when they are used the next time. Pre-treating the water helps prevent this. I have frequently used a charcoal filter system to insure safe, good tasting water after chemical treatment.

Another filtration method is perhaps one of the oldest, namely filtering through unglazed ceramic material. This was done in large crocks — a slow filtration method popular in tropical countries many years ago. A modern version of this old system is the development of a pressurized pump method. Made in Switzerland, the Katadyn Pocket Filter has a ceramic core inclosed in a tough plastic housing, fitted with an aluminum pump. The built in pump forces water through the ceramic filter at a rate of approximately 3/4 ths a quart per minute. Turbid water will plug the filter, but a brush is provided to easily restore full flow rates. This filter has a .2 micron size, which eliminates all bacteria and larger pathogens. Pre-treating of the water is not required. There is evidence that viral particles are also killed by this unit as the ceramic material is silver impregnated which appears to denaturate virus as they pass through the filter. This possibility is being evaluated by the FDA at this time. I have worked with many groups using this device and they have had many favorable comments. These units are not cheap, costing about $200.00 retail. They weigh 23 ounces.

Another method of water purification has been with us a long time, namely using our old friend fire. Bringing water to a boil will effectively kill pathogens and make water safe to drink. One reads variously to boil water 5, 10, even 20 minutes. But simply bringing the water temperature to 150°F (65.5°C) is adequate to kill the pathogens discussed above, and all others besides. At high altitude the boiling point of water is reduced. For example, at 25,000 feet the boiling point of water would be about 185°F (85°C).

This matter of the minimal length of time required to make water safe to drink should be discussed further. Bringing water to a boil is the minimal safe time for preparation. At times fuel or water supply may be in short supply and this minimal time must be used. It will never be necessary to boil water longer than 5 minutes and the shortest time mentioned (ie just bringing the water to a boil) will suffice for a safe drinking water. This water will not be sterile, but it will be safe to drink.

Water may be obtained by squeezing any fresh water fish and from some plants. Never drink urine or sea water, as the high solute content of these liquids will only dehydrate you more and make the problem worse. A solar still can be prepared for reprocessing urine, water from grass, etc. — as indicated in *Figure* 13. In water poor areas, catching rain water may be an essential part of routine survival. Be careful of melting ice: treat all ice melt water as indicated above. There is a very strong chance of contamination of ice deposits.

SOLAR STILL

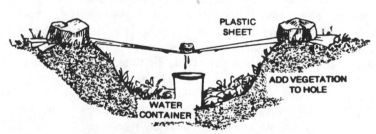

FIGURE 13. SOLAR STILL CONDENSING DRINKABLE WATER FROM VEGETATION OR CONTAMINATED SOURCES

HUMAN WASTE DISPOSAL — This is not only a matter of esthetics, but of primary preventative medicine. Improper waste disposal on the wagon trains heading west in 1840-1850's caused vast epidemics of cholera in the trains that followed. Unbelievable numbers of people were killed. Even in our wilderness areas, it is widely acknowledged that the cleanest appearing streams are suspect of human contamination. Most official campsites in the national park system have toilets constructed. These should *always* be used. Otherwise, human defecation should be buried at least 40 yards from a lake shore or stream run-off. Waste should be buried shallow, allowing rapid decomposition. Use biodegradeable toilet paper, such as one would buy from a camping specialty store or for use in septic tanks. An inexpensive lightweight plastic trowel, ideal for digging a "cat hole," can be purchased at most specialty shops. For an expanded discussion of this topic, see Calvin Rutstrum's *CHIPS FROM A WILDERNESS LOG,* Pages 73-76.

CONSTIPATION — One of the currently popular wilderness medical texts has instructions on how to break up a fecal impaction digitally (i.e., using your finger to break up a hard stool stuck in the rectum). Don't let it get that far. In healthy young adults (especially teenagers), there may be a reluctance to defecate in the wilderness due to the unusual surroundings, lack of a toilet and perhaps swarms of insects or freezing cold. It is the group leader's responsibility to *make sure* that a trip member does not fecal hoard — i.e., fail to defecate in a reasonable length of time. Certainly one should be concerned after 3 days of no bowel movements.

To prevent this problem, I always include a stewed fruit at breakfast. The use of hot and cold in the morning will frequently wake up the "gastric-colic reflex" and get things moving perfectly well. If the 5-day mark is approaching, especially if the patient — and they *have* become a patient at about this point — is obviously uncomfortable, it may become necessary to use a laxative. From the medical kit (non RX item) give 1 bisacodyl laxative tablet 5 mg at bedtime. If that fails, the next morning take 2 of the tablets. Under winter conditions, when getting up in sub-zero weather might prove abominable, or under heavy insect conditions, take these tablets in the morning, rather than at night, to preclude this massive inconvenience. Any laxative will cause abdominal cramping, depending upon how strong it is. Be expecting this.

HEMORRHOIDS (PILES) — These are a type of varicose vein around the rectum. External hemorrhoids are small, rounded purplish masses which enlarge when straining at stool. Unless a clot forms in them, they are soft and nontender. when clots form, they can become very painful, actually excruciating. Hemorrhoids are the most common cause of rectal bleeding, with the blood also appearing on the toilet tissue. The condition can be very painful for about 5 days, after which the clots starts to absorb, the pain decreases and the mass regresses, leaving only small skin tags. Provide the patient with pain medication (non Rx mobigesic, 2 tablets every 4 hours or, Rx Tylenol #3, 1 or 2 tablets every 4 hours). The application of heat is helpful during the acute phase. Heat a cloth in water and apply for 15 minutes 4 times a day if possible. Avoid constipation, as mentioned in that section.

Apply the Dibucaine ointment every 4 hours from the non-Rx oral/topical hit for local pain relief.

MENSTRUAL PROBLEMS — Menstrual flow is best contained with a vaginally inserted pad, but be sure to have had experience with the chosen product prior to heading backcountry. Most come with waxed disposable paper bags, but an inner bag of plastic should be carried if it will be necessary to pack out discarded pads. The Surgipad from the topical bandaging unit will substitute as an outer sanitary napkin if none is available. Menstrual cramping can generally be controlled with Mobigesic 1 or 2 tablets every 4 to 6 hours from the nonRx kit. From the Rx kit, if necessary, one could use Tylenol #3, 1 tablet every 4 to 6 hours. A prescription product that I have had considerable success in prescribing for this condition is Nalfon, 600 mg. 1 tablet every 6 hours as required. It is designed as an anti-arthritic, but its anti-prostaglandin activities make it a theoretical, as well as practical, pharmacologic agent with great promise in this area. A good non Rx item is Sunril, 1 capsule every 6 hours, maximum use is 10 days in a one month period.

Menorrhagia, either excessive flow or long period of flowage, should be evaluated by a physician to determine if there is an underlying pathology that could or should be corrected. If the problem is simply one of hormone imbalance, this can frequently be corrected with the use of birth control pills with higher amounts of estrogen and lower progestogen content. Again, the physician should be consulted well in advance of the wilderness outing, so that these symptoms will have been brought under control by the time of the expedition.

HERNIA — The most common hernia in a male is the inguinal hernia, which is an outpouching of the intestines through a weak area in the abdominal wall located above and on either side of the penis. A hernia can be produced while straining, either lifting, coughing, sneezing, etc. There will be a sharp pain at the location of the hernia and the patient will note a bulge. This bulge may disappear when he lies on his back and relaxes (i.e. the hernia has reduced). If the intestine in the hernia is squeezed by the abdominal wall to the point that the blood supply is cut off, the hernia is termed a "strangulated" hernia. This is a medical emergency, as the loop of gut in the hernia will die, turn gangrenous, and lead to a generalized peritonitis or abdomen infection — as discussed under APPENDICITIS. This condition is much worse than an appendicitis and death will result if not treat surgically.

The hernia that fails to reduce, or disappear when the victim relaxes in a recumbent position, is termed "incarcerated". While this may turn into an emergency, it is not one at that point. Most hernia caused by straining in adults will not strangulate. Further straining should be avoided. If lifting items is *necessary*, or while coughing, etc., the victim should protect himself from further tissue damage by pressing against the area with one hand — thus holding the hernia in reduction. It would be a rather awkward way to carry a canoe.

BLADDER INFECTION — The hallmarks of bladder infection (cystitis) are the urge to urinate frequently, burning upon urination, small amounts of urine being voided with each passage, discomfort in the suprapubic region — the lowest area of the abdomen. Frequently the victim has fever with its attendant chills and muscle ache. In fact, people can become quite ill with a generalized infection caused by numerous bacteria entering their blood stream. At times the urine becomes cloudy and even bloody. Cloudy urine without the above symptoms does NOT mean an infection is present and is frequently normal. The infection can extend to the kidney, at which time the patient also has considerable flank pain, centered at the bottom edge of the ribs along the lateral aspect of the back on the involved side (often both sides). Bladder infections are more common in women than men, they are not an uncommon problem in either sex. One suffering from recurrent infections should be thoroughly evaluated by a physician prior to an extended wilderness trip.

There have been many drugs developed for treating infections of the genito-urinary system. The antibiotics recommended for the Rx medical kits all work excellently here. Bactrim DS taken 1 tablet twice daily, or the doxycycline 100 mg taken 1 tablet twice daily are very effective. Generally 5 days is a sufficient length of time for treatment. Symptoms should disappear within 24 to 48 hours, or it may mean that the bacteria is resistant to the antibiotic and the other should be substituted. For severe infections, with high fever which has not responded within 48 hours to oral antibiotic use, the injectable Rocephin 1 gm IM given daily in place of the oral antibiotic would be a superior choice.

Additional treatment should consist of drinking copious amounts of fluid, at least 8 quarts per day! At times this simple rinsing action may even cure a cystitis, but I wouldn't want to count on it if an antibiotic were available. Discomfort may be relieved by Mobigesic from the non-Rx supplies, or Tylenol #3 for the Rx Oral/Topical kit, but these are seldom required due to the rapid onset of relief following adminis-tration of the antibiotic. The Mobigesic may be needed to treat the fever which accompanies such problems prior to the start of the antibiotic and during the early stages of therapy.

VENEREAL DISEASE — is totally preventable by abstention, any other technique falls short of being foolproof. Most venereal infections cause symptoms in the male, but frequently do not in the female. Either may note increased discomfort with urination, the development of sores or unusual growths around the genitalia, and discharge from the portions of the anatomy used in sex (pharynx, penis, vagina, anus). Some venereal diseases can be very difficult to detect, such as syphilis, hepatitis B, and AIDS. Hepatitis B is rampant in many parts of the world with high carrier rates in local population groups. It can be prevented with a vaccine (see Appendix A). There are no vaccines against the other venereal diseases.

Gonorrhea is common and easy to detect in the male. The appearance of symptoms is from 2 to 8 days from time of contact and basically consists of a copious greenish-yellow discharge. The female will frequently not have symptoms. From the Rx kit provide doxycycline 100 mg twice daily for 15 days, to ensure adequate treatment of syphilis.

Syphilis has an incubation period of 2 to 6 weeks before the characteristic sore appears. The development of a painless ulcer (¼ to ½ inch in size), generally with enlarged, non-tender lymph nodes in the region, is a hallmark of this disease. A painful ulcer formation is more characteristic of herpes simplex. The lesion may not appear in a syphilis victim, making the early detection of this disease very difficult. A second stage consisting of a generalized skin rash (generally which does not itch, does not produce blisters, and frequently appears on the soles of the feet and palms of the hands) appears about 6 weeks after the lesions mentioned above. The third phase of the disease may develop in several years, during which nearly any organ system in the body may be affected. The overall study of syphilis is so complicated that a great medical instructor once said, "To know syphilis is to know medicine." Treatment of primary stage syphilis is 15 days of antibiotic, as mentioned above.

Development of a clear, scanty discharge in the male may be due to chlamydia or other nonspecific urethral infections. Symptoms appear 7 to 28 days after contact. Women may have no symptoms. Treat with the doxycycline 100 mg twice daily for 15 days. Blood tests for syphilis should be performed before treatment and again in 3 months. 20% of victims with nonspecific urethritis will have a relapse, therefore adequate medical follow-up after the trip is essential.

The herpes lesions can respond to Zovirax ointment applied frequently during the day until they disappear in 8 to 10 days. Zovirax capsules 200 mg taken 5 times daily for 10 days are effective during the acute phase.

Upon return home, trip members who may have experienced a sexual disease should be seen by their physician for serology tests for syphilis, hepatitis B tests, chlamydial smears, gonorrheal cultures, herpes simplex titers, and possibly HIV studies for AIDS. Lesions or growths should be examined as possible molluscum contagiosum and venereal warts should be treated.

PAINFUL TESTICLE — If caused by trauma provide support by having the victim lay down on insulated ground with a cloth draped over both thighs, forming a sling or cradle on which the painful scrotum may rest. If ambulatory, provide support to prevent movement of the scrotum. Cold packs would help initially and providing adequate pain and nausea medication as available is certainly appropriate. Antibiotic is not required unless a fever results.

Spontaneous pain in the scrotum, with enlargement of a testicle can be due to infection of the testicle (orchitis) or more commonly to the sperm collecting system called the epididymis (epididymitis). Treatment of choice would be to provide antibiotic such as the doxycycline 100 mg 1 tablet twice daily, which is frequently employed for this problem. The Bactrim DS 1 tablet twice daily is also frequently used. Pain medication should be provided as necessary.

The problem may not be due to an infection at all — it is possible for the testicle to become twisted, due to a slight congenital defect, with severe pain resulting. This "testicular torsion," as it is called, is a surgical emergency. It can be almost impossible to distinguish from orchitis. In a suspected case of torsion it is helpful to try to reduce the torsion. Since the testicle always seems to rotate "inward" one need only rotate the affected testicle "outward." This will often result in immediate relief of the pain. If one cannot achieve this, or if you are dealing with an orchitis, no harm is done; but if it is a torsion you have saved the testicle and the trip. A person with severe testicular pain should be evacuated as soon as possible as infection or torsion can result in sterility of the involved side. An unreduced testicular torsion can become gangrenous with life threatening infection resulting.

VAGINAL DISCHARGE AND ITCHING — This is frequently not a venereal disease. The most common cause is fungal or *monilia* infection. This condition is more common in conditions of high humidity or with the wearing of tight clothes such as pants or panty hose.

A typical monilia infection has a copious white discharge with curds like cottage cheese. From the nonRx Oral/Topical Unit one can use the miconazole 2% cream. This formulation has been designed for foot and other skin fungal problems, but it will work vaginally as well.

A frothy greenish-yellow, irritating discharge may be due to Trichomonas infection. This can be spread by sexual encounters. The male infected with this organism generally has no symptoms, or a slight mucoid discharge early in the morning, noted before urinating. The treatment of choice is Flagyl (metronidazole) 250 mg capsule 3 times a day for 10 days, or 8 capsules given as one dose. This drug cannot be taken with alcohol. Sexual abstention is important until medication is finished and a cure is evident clinically. Flagyl was not included in the recommended medical kit.

A copious yellow-green discharge may be gonorrhea. Any irritating discharge that is not thick and white is best treated with antibiotic such as the doxycycline or Bactrim DS. Treat for 5 days. If sexual contact may have been the source of the problem, treat for 15 days. A douche of very dilute Hibiclens surgical scrub, or very dilute detergent solution, can be prepared and may be helpful. Very dilute is better than too strong. Frequent douching is not required, but may be used daily for a while as required for comfort and hygiene.

LACERATIONS — Wound care, whether in the wilderness or not, can be broken into chronological phases. The first phase consists of SAVING THE VICTIM'S LIFE — by stopping the bleeding and treating for shock. Even if the victim is not bleeding, you will want to treat for shock. Shock has many fancy medical definitions, but on the bottom line it amounts to an inadequate oxygenated blood supply getting to the brain. Lay the patient down, elevate feet above the head, and provide protection from the environment — from both the ground and the atmosphere. Grab anything which you can find for this at first — use jackets, pack frames, unrolled tents, whatever.

Direct pressure is the best method of stopping bleeding — in fact pressure alone can stop bleeding from amputated limbs! When the accident first occurs, you may even need to use your bare hand to stem the flow of blood. With the blood stopped, even with your hand, and the victim on the ground in the shock treatment position, the actual emergency is over. Their life is safe. And you have bought time to gather together various items you need to perform the definitive job of caring for this wound. You have also treated for psychogenic shock — the shock of "fear". For obviously someone knows what to do: they have taken charge, they have stopped the bleeding, they are giving orders to gather materials together. This shock caused by fear is frequently more of a problem than that caused by loss of blood — or hypovolemia.

In the first aid management of this wound, the next step is simply bandaging and then transporting the victim to professional medical care. For those isolated in the wilderness who must provide long term care for wounds, further management will go through several more phases: cleaning, closing, dressing, and treating complications of infection that could happen.

After saving the person's life by stopping the bleeding and treating for shock, ADEQUATE CLEANSING is the most important aspect of would management. Especially when in an isolated or survival situation, the prevention of infection is of critical importance, and this can only be assured by aggressive cleansing techniques.

There is an adage in nature: "The solution to pollution is dilution." In wound care this means copious irrigation. The use of a bota bag or a water cube to provide a strong force of water is very helpful. A source of adequately clean water may be of concern. Frankly, this water does not need to be potable, or drinkable, for the bacteria that would cause harm in your intestines are generally not the ones that cause most wound infections. Certainly avoid silty waters or water with organic debris, for water with high levels of particulate matter is very apt to be contaminated with higher levels of bacteria. The whole purpose of scrubbing a wound is to reduce the total number of potentially harmful bacteria. We won't get 'em all out, but if the total number is sufficiently small, the body's own defense mechanisms can take over and finish the job for us. See page 79 for techniques of water purification.

Besides irrigation, there is a technique of cleaning used by physicians in the operating room called "debridement." This amounts to cutting away destroyed tissue. Of course, there is no way a person can do this in the bush — especially with inadequate lighting, equipment, and training. But we CAN safely approximate it by vigorously rubbing the area with a piece of sterile gauze. The rigorous scrubbing action will remove blood clot, torn bits of tissue, pieces of foreign bodies — all items which generally result in higher bacteria counts or foci for bacterial growth.

This scrubbing process has to be accomplished quickly — it is painful and the victim will not tolerate it for long. Have everything ready: clean, dry dressings to apply afterward; the water supply; an instrument to spread the wound open (a splinter forcep is ideal); and sterile gauze to use for scrubbing this wound. Once everything is ready, and assistance is at hand (perhaps someone to help direct the jet of water into the wound, another to assist shooing the blackflies away or comfort the victim), go to it! If this job is performed well, the final outcome will be great. This part of wound care is far more important than wound closure technique. It will be messy. And it will hurt. But spread the wound apart, blast that water in there, scrub briskly with the gauze pad. This whole process will have to be completed in 20 to 30 seconds. In the operating room, or under local anesthesia in the emergency room, we might take 15 minutes or longer. You won't be able to take that much time, but you must be thorough and vigorous. When in doubt, do more — if the patient can tolerate it within reason.

Once completed with irrigation, the wound will be bleeding vigorously again — the blood clots having been knocked off during the cleansing process. Apply a sterile dressing and use direct pressure to again stop the bleeding. Use direct pressure as long as necessary to stop bleeding. Five to ten minutes usually suffice, but if an hour or more is required keep at it!

With direct pressure still applied, dry around the wound. We are ready to now enter the WOUND CLOSURE PHASE of wound care. Perhaps more worry and concern exists about this phase of wound care than the others, but it is really the easiest — and much less important than the first two phases just discussed.

If the laceration can be held together with tape, by all means use tape as the definitive treatment. Butterfly bandages are universally available, and generally work very well. The commercial butterflies are superior to homemade in that they are packaged sterile with a no-stick center portion. They can be made in the field by cutting and folding the center edges in to cover the adhesive in the very center of short tape strips, thus avoiding adhesive contact with the wound. Of course such homemade strips will not be sterile, but in general they will be very adequate.

An improvement in the butterfly bandage was the Steri-Strip by the 3-M Corp. I feel that today the best tape wound closure made is the Cover-Strip by Beiersdorf, Inc. These strips drain fluid more readily and stick more firmly than Steri-Strips. Even better for amateur wound closers, they can be pulled off and re-applied when tyring to correctly close the wound. Steri-Strips loose all of their stick once pulled up. If one end is pulled up to reposition it, then that strip is ruined.

In applying any type of tape closure, the best technique is to pinch the wound together as the strips are being applied. That could take two people to accomplish. A simple one person method is to fasten a strip of tape to one edge of the wound and then fasten the next strip of tape to the other edge. Then approximate the wound edges by pulling on the tapes and fasten them down.

A new method of holding skin edges together is with the use of stainless steel staples. A special disposable device will contain a certain number of sterile staples which rapidly staple the wound edges while pinching the wound together. This obviously stings while being used, but the pain is brief and the wound is secure. A very useful such device is the Precise Five-Shot by 3-M Corp, which obviously contains 5 staples. A special disposable staple remover is very handy for taking staples out virtually painlessly. The skin stapler and staple remover are non-Rx. They come packaged in sterile, water-proof containers.

If taping will not hold the wound closed — and this may be the case when a stretch is placed frequently on the wound due to its location, or to a gap due to missing tissue — then it will have to be sutured (stitched). Suture material is available in many forms and with many types of needles.

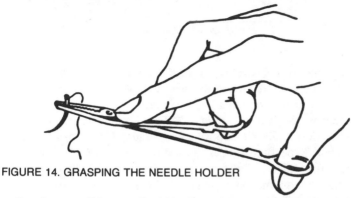

FIGURE 14. GRASPING THE NEEDLE HOLDER

For the expedition medical kit, I would recommend using 3-0 nylon suture with a curved pre-attached needle. This comes in a sterile packet ready for use. It will be necessary to use a needle holder to properly use this suture. The needle holder looks like a pair of scissors, but it has a flat surface with grooves that grab the needle and a lock device that holds the needle firmly. It is held as illustrated (see *Figure 14*) to steady the hand.

FIGURE 15. PROPER PLACEMENT OF SUTURE

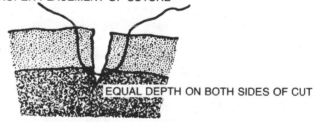

EQUAL DEPTH ON BOTH SIDES OF CUT

Apply pressure in the direction of the needle, namely twist your wrist in such a manner that the needle will pass directly into the skin and cleanly penetrate, following through with the motion to allow the needle to curve through the subcutaneous tissue and sweep upward and through the skin on the other side of the wound. (Note illustration *Figure 15*).

FIGURE 16. IMPROPER PLACEMENT OF SUTURE

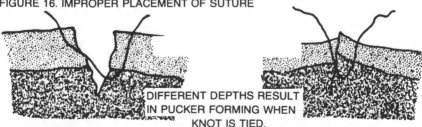

DIFFERENT DEPTHS RESULT IN PUCKER FORMING WHEN KNOT IS TIED.

It is important to have the needle enter both sides of the wound at the same depth or the wound will not pull together evenly and there will be a pucker if the needle took a deep bite on one side and a shallow bite on the other (see *Figure 16*).

A square knot is tied with the use of the needle holder in a very easy manner. Loop the suture around the needle holder once, using the long end of the thread (see *Figure 17A*), then grasp the short end and pull the wound together (*Figure 17B and C*). Then loop the long end around the needle holder again the opposite way (*Figure 17F*). This will form a square knot. Repeat this process a third time in the original direction to insure a firm knot. Do not pull too tightly as this will pucker the skin, just an approximation is required. Frankly, a knot tied in any fashion will do perfectly well.

These stitches should not be placed too closely together — usually, on the limbs and body 4 stitches per inch will suffice. On the face, however, use 6 per inch. Here it is best to use 5-0 nylon, as it will minimize scar formation from the needle and suture. I use a 6-0 suture on the face, but it is considerably more difficult to use than the 5-0. The use of these stitches can be augmented with tape strips or butterfly closures to help hold the wound together and to cut down on the number of stitches required. Once they are in, leave stitches in the limbs for 10 days, in the trunk and scalp for 7 days, and in the face for 4 days.

Special Considerations — It has been found that shaving an area increases the chance of wound infection. Scalp lacerations are hard to suture when unshaven due to the matting of hair with blood and accidental incorporation of hair into the wound. However, catching hair in the wound is not detrimental. Just pull it loose from the wound with a pair of forceps or tweezers when you are through suturing. Scalp wounds bleed excessively — be expecting this. Spurting blood vessels can be clamped with a hemostat and tied off with a piece of the 3-0 gut suture recommended for the field surgical kit. To tie, simply place a knot in the flesh to fall beneath the tip of the hemostat. Someone may have to remove the hemostat while you are cinching the first loop of the knot. Or you may simply suture the scalp wound closed and apply pressure between each suture to minimize intra-operative bleeding. Apply firm direct pressure after suturing to minimize hematoma — or blood pocket formation from bleeding within the wound.

Anywhere on the body you will note that entrance and exit points of the needle puncture will bleed quite freely. A little pressure always causes this bleeding to stop — it is not necessary to delay your sewing to even worry about it. Just apply pressure until this bleeding from the needle punctures stops, cleanse the skin when you are done to remove dried blood, and dress the wound.

If sewing an eyebrow or the vermillion border of the lip, approximate the edges first with a suture before sewing the ends or other portion of the laceration. Never shave an eyebrow. Use the 5-0 nylon suture on

FIGURE 17. FORMING A SQUARE KNOT USING A NEEDLE HOLDER

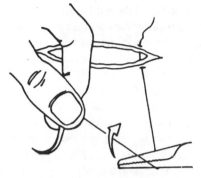

FIGURE 17-A. LOOP HOLDER

FIGURE 17-B. GRASP END
THROUGH LOOP

FIGURE 17-C. PULL TIGHT

FIGURE 17-D. LOOP HOLDER
IN REVERSE

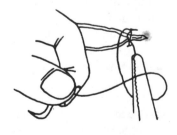

FIGURE 17-E. GRASP END
THROUGH LOOP

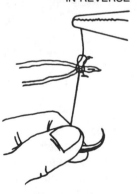

FIGURE 17-F. PULL TIGHT

the face and remove these sutures in 4 days, replacing them with strips of tape at that time.

When sewing the inside of the mouth, use the 3-0 gut suture. These sutures tend to unwind very easily, especially if the patient cannot resist touching them with their tongue. When making the knot, tie it over and over. As the mouth heals rapidly, if the sutures come out within a day, the laceration has generally stopped bleeding and may hold itself together without further help. These mouth sutures will generally dissolve on their own, but remaining ones can be removed within 4 days.

Lacerations on the tongue can almost always be left alone. The wound may appear ugly for a few days, but within a week or two there will be remarkable healing. Infections in the tongue or mouth from cuts are very rare. If the edge of a tongue is *badly* lacerated, so that the tongue is cut 1/4 the way across or more, then sewing the edge together is warranted. Use the 3-0 gut suture. See also page 41.

Suture through the skin surface only and avoid important structures underneath. If tendon or nerve damage has occurred, irrigate the wound thoroughly as described above and repair the skin with either tape or sutures as necessary. The tendon, etc., can be repaired by a surgeon upon return to the outside — weeks later if necessary. If a delayed repair is necessary after a tendon laceration, the surgeon would probably wait a week to insure that a wound infection is not going to develop before attempting further surgery.

For anesthesia you will require a Rx to obtain injectable lidocaine 1% and a syringe with needle. Inject through the wound, just under the skin on both sides of the cut. Cleansing and suturing soon after a cut may help minimize the pain, due to tissue "shock" in the immediate post-trauma period. Ice applied to the wound area can help numb the pain, but local topical anesthetic agents like dibucaine are of no help in pain control. Two Mobigesic or 1 or 2 Tylenol #3, given about 1 hour prior to surgery, may help minimize pain.

The number of sutures that are required can be minimized by placing Cover-Strips (or butterfly strips, etc), between sutures. A wound that tends to break open due to tension, such as over the knee, can be stabilized by splinting the joint so that it cannot move while the wound is healing.

Most sutured lacerations will leak a little blood during the first 24 hours. The ideal covering would be the Nu-Gauze pads as mentioned on page 5. After the wound becomes dry, the Tegaderm dressing (page 5) will keep the sutures visible and the wound protected even if it must get submersed in water. Wounds that are leaking considerable serum and/or blood should be covered by Spenco 2nd Skin and managed as discussed on page 43.

Antibiotic Use — It is always tempting to place a person on antibiotic after a laceration, but I would advise against doing this unless the wound was from an animal or human bite (page 97), or involved an open fracture (page 111). Bacteria are jealous creatures and do not like to share their food source with other species. If an infection were to develop, it will generally be a pure culture, the other species that originally contaminated the wound having been killed off by the body defense mechanisms and the winning bacterium. If the patient is on an antibiotic from the beginning, the winning bacterium is guaranteed to be resistant to your medication. If no antibiotic was used initially, then there is hope that the emergent bacterium will be sensitive to the antibiotic which you are about to employ.

WOUND INFECTION AND INFLAMMATION — Lacerations which have been cleaned and either sutured, taped, or stapled together will generally become slightly inflamed. Inflammation is part of the healing process and does not indicate infection, yet the appearance is similar. It is a matter of degree. The hallmarks of infection are: swelling, warmth to touch, reddish color, and pain. Inflammation has slight swelling and reddish color. If the cut has a reddish swelling that extends beyond ¼ inch from the wound edge, infection has probably started.

The method of treatment of wound infection is quite simple. Remove some of the tapes (sutures or staples) and allow the wound to open and drain. Apply warm, moist compresses for 15 to 20 minutes every 2 hours. This will promote drainage of the wound and increase the local circulation, thus bringing large numbers of friendly white blood cells and fibroblasts into the area. The fibroblast tries to wall off the infection and prevent further spread of the germs. Once an infection has obviously started, the use of an antibiotic will be helpful — but not always essential. From the Rx Oral/Topical Unit use the doxycycline 100 mg twice daily. If the Rx Injectable Unit is available, use the Rocephin 500 mg twice daily IM.

CELLULITIS — is a very dangerous and rapidly progressive skin infection which results in the reddish swelling of the skin without pus or blister formation. The lesion spreads by the hour, with streaks of red progressing ahead of the swelling toward the heart. This represents the travel of infection along the lymphatic system and is frequently called "blood poisoning" in the vernacular. While lymphatic spread is not strictly blood poisoning, cellulitis does frequently lead to generalized blood poisoning (septicemia) and can cause the development of chills, fever and other symptoms of generalized profound infection such as lethargy and even shock. Very dangerous and virulent germs are responsible. Strong antibiotics are necessary. The application of local heat is very helpful. Old time remedies included the use of various "drawing salves," but nothing works better than local hot compresses. Local heat increases the circulation of blood into the infected area, bringing white cells which kill the bacteria directly and which also produce antibodies to aid in the killing process. The infection fighters and the walling off process of the fibroblasts will hopefully contain and destroy the infection. When this walling off process succeeds, then an abscess is formed (see next section). If the Rx Injectable Unit is available, give Rocephin 1 gm IM, followed by 500 mg twice daily. If the Rx Oral/Topical Unit is available, give doxycycline 100 mg, 2 immediately, followed by 1 twice daily.

ABSCESS — An abscess (boil, furuncle) is a pocket of pus (white blood cells), germs, and red blood cells that have been contained by an envelope of scar tissue produced by fibroblasts. This protects the body from further spread of the germs. It is part of the body's strong natural defense against invasion by bacteria. Conversely, many antibiotics cannot penetrate into the abscess cavity very well. The cure of an abscess is surgical. They must be opened and drained. There are two basic ways in which this can happen. First, moist warm soaks will not only aid in abscess formation, but will also aid in bringing the infection to the surface and cause the infection to "ripen," even open and drain on its own. An abscess can be very painful and this opening period very prolonged. Once the abscess is on the surface it is generally better to open it using a technique called "incision and drainage" or I&D. The ideal instrument for an I&D is a #11 scalpel blade. This thin stab blade will penetrate the surface skin and open the cavity with minimal pressure on the wound. (See *Figure 3,* page 11.)

Abscesses are very painful, primarily because of the pressure within them. A person coming into a doctor's office with a painful abscess would expect to have it anesthetized before opening. But injections into these areas only add to the pain. The best anesthesia is to cool the wound area. In the field an ice cube or application of an instant cold pack will help provide some anesthesia. A person with a painful abscess will quite frankly let you try the knife as they can become desperate for pain relief. The relief that they get when the pressure is removed is immediate — even without cooling. Coat the skin surface around the abscess with triple antibiotic ointment from the non-Rx Topical Bandaging Unit, to protect the skin from the bacteria that are draining from the wound. Spread of infection from these bacteria is unlikely, however, unless the skin is abraded or otherwise broken.

FRICTION BLISTERS — will normally require opening as they have formed on areas where packs, shoes or other equipment is rubbing. These can be prevented and treated with Spenco 2nd Skin as indicated on pages 5 and 43. When opening, cleanse the area with soap or surgical scrub. An application of triple antibiotic ointment will ensure sterile conditions. A sterile piece of Spenco 2nd Skin, held on with Spenco Adhesive Knit Bandage will allow a severe friction blister to heal even while the trip continues using the same new shoes that caused the problem in the first place.

PUNCTURE WOUND — Allow these to bleed, thus hoping to effect an automatic irrigation of bacteria from the wound. Apply suction with the Extractor (venom suction device) immediately and continue the vacuum for 20 to 30 minutes. Cleanse the wound area with surgical scrub — soapy water — and apply triple antibiotic ointment to the surrounding skin surface. Do not tape shut, but rather start warm compress applications for 20 minutes, every 2 hours for the next 1 to 2 days, or until it is apparent that no sub-surface infection has started. These soaks should be as warm as the patient can tolerate without danger of burning the skin. Larger pieces of cloth work best — such as undershirts — as they hold the heat longer. Infection can be prevented, or treated, with antibiotics as described in the section on cellulitis above. Dressing should be with a clean cloth. If sterile items are in short supply they need not be used on this type of wound. Tetanus immunization should be within 5 years.

ABRASIONS — An abrasion is the loss of surface skin due to a scraping injury. The best treatment is cleansing with Hibiclens surgical scrub, application of triple antibiotic ointment, and the use of Spenco 2nd Skin with Adhesive Knit Bandage — all components of the Non-Rx Topical Bandaging Unit. This type of wound leaks profusely, but the above bandaging allows rapid healing, excellent protection, and considerable pain relief. Avoid the use of alcohol on these wounds as it tends to damage the tissue, to say nothing of causing excessive pain. Lacking first aid supplies, cleanse gently with mild detergent and protect from dirt, bugs, etc., the best that you can. Tetanus immunization should be within 10 years.

HUMAN BITES — Unless group discipline has really degenerated, human bites are due to accidents such as falling and puncturing flesh with teeth. Bites within the victim's own mouth seldom become infected and are discussed under lacerations. Human bites anywhere else have the highest infection rate of any wound. Scrub vigorously with Hibiclens surgical scrub, soapy water, or any other antiseptic that you can find. Pick out broken teeth or other debris. Use the Extractor for 20 to 30 minutes, further use will not help. Coat the wound area with triple antibiotic ointment. Start the application of hot, wet compresses as described under puncture wounds. Start antibiotic with Rocephin 1 gm IM every 24 hours, or from the Rx Oral/Topical kit use doxycycline 100 mg, 2 now and then 1 every 12 hours. Tetanus immunization must be within 5 years. Bite wounds to the hand are extremely serious and should be seen by a qualified hand surgeon as soon as possible.

ANIMAL BITES — Animal bite lacerations must be vigorously cleaned, but hot soaks need not be started initially. Most authorities state that bite lacerations should not be taped or sutured closed due to an increased incidence of wound infection. This has not been my personal experience, nor that of many ER physicians with whom I have discussed this problem. After vigorous wound cleansing I would close gaping wounds as described under LACERATIONS. Puncture wounds should not be closed, only gaping wounds. If an infection seems to start, treat as indicated in the section on wound infection on page 95 by removing the closures and starting hot soaks and antibiotics. Tetanus immunization must be current within 5 years.

RABIES — Can be transmitted on the North American continent by several species of mammals, namely skunk, bat, fox, coyote, racoon, bobcat, and wolf. Obviously, if removing an animal from a trap, separating mother from child, or taking food from a critter causes an attack, the most likely cause is not rabies. An attack by a wounded animal is cause for concern, as the animal may be wounded due to loss of coordination from rabies. Any unprovoked attack by one of these mammals should be considered an attack by a rabid animal. Dogs and cats in the United States have a low incidence of rabies. Information from local departments of health will indicate if rabies is currently of concern in these animals. In many foreign countries the bite of a cat or dog should be considered rabid. Animals whose bites have never caused rabies in humans in the US are livestock (cattle, sheep, horse), rabbit, gerbil, chipmunk, squirrel, rat, and mouse. Hawaii is the only rabies free state. Countries free of rabies are England, Australia, Japan, and parts of the Caribbean. In Europe the red fox is the animal most often rabid with documented cases spreading to dogs, cats, cattle, and deer. Canada's rabies occurs mostly in foxes and skunks in the province of Ontario. Mongoose rabies is found in South Africa and the Caribbean islands of Cuba, Puerto Rico, Hispaniola, and Grenada. In the United States there have been 9 cases of rabies reported between 1980 and 1987. In India

40,000 to 50,000 people die yearly from rabies, with an equal incidence in the other developing counties of Asia, Africa, and Latin America.

The treatment for rabies is prophylaxis with Rabies Immune Globulin 20 IU/kg with half infiltrated around the wound and the remaining half in the gluteal area (upper outer quadrant of the bottom) and human diploid cell vaccine (HDCV) 1 ml given IM in the shoulder on days 0, 3, 7, 14, and 28.

The incubation period in a human is 1 to 2 months. Rabies is a vicious disease that is usually fatal once it clinically develops. Because of this, there is generous use of rabies vaccine and immune globulin. Approximately 20,000 people are vaccinated here yearly to prevent this disease. Persons having to work with potentially rabid animal populations can be immunized with the vaccine and given yearly booster shots. It is possible to obtain the disease by merely being contaminated with the saliva or blood of an infected animal if it comes in contact with a break in the skin or mucous membranes — possibly even by breathing in dust infected with the virus (such as in an infected cave).

FISHHOOK REMOVAL — A fishhook should be taped into place and not removed if there is any danger of causing damage to nearby or underlying structures or if the patient is uncooperative. Cut the fish line off the hook, but do not cut the hook close to the skin with your wire cutters. This makes subsequent manipulation by the surgeon more difficult. There are three basic methods of removing a fishhook.

Push through, snip off method: While the technique seems straight forward, consider a few points: 1) Pushing the hook should not endanger underlying or adjacent structures. This limits the technique's usefulness, but it is still frequently an easy, quick method to employ. 2) Skin is not easy to push through. It is very elastic and will tent up over the barb as you try to push it through. Place side-cutting wire cutters, with jaws spread apart, over the point on the surface where you expect the hook point to punch through. 3) This is a painful process, and skin hurts when being poked from the bottom up, as much as from the top down. Once committed, get the push through portion of this project over with in a hurry. 4) This adds a second puncture wound to the victim's anatomy. Cleanse the skin at the anticipated penetration site before shoving the hook through using soap or a surgical scrub. 5) When snipping the protruding point off, cover the wound area with your free hand to protect you and others from the flying hook point. Otherwise you may need to refer to the section on "removing foreign bodies from the eye." The steps are simple: A) Push the hook through, B) snip it off, C) back the barbless hook out, D) treat the puncture wounds.

The string jerk method: works best in areas with little connective tissue in the involved area. Fingers are loaded with fibrous tissue that tends to hinder a smooth hook removal. This technique works best in the back of the head, the shoulder, and most aspects of the torso, arms, and legs. It is highly useful and can be virtually painless, causing minimal trauma.

FIGURE 18. THE STRING JERK METHOD OF REMOVING A FISHHOOK

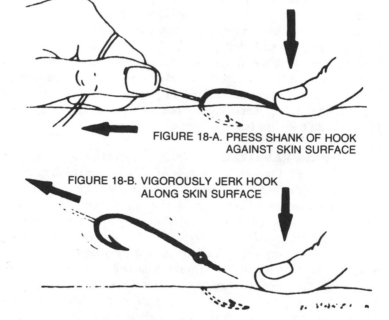

FIGURE 18-A. PRESS SHANK OF HOOK
AGAINST SKIN SURFACE

FIGURE 18-B. VIGOROUSLY JERK HOOK
ALONG SKIN SURFACE

Important to the method is looping a line, such as the fish line, around the hook and insuring that this line is held flush against the skin. Pushing down on the eye portion of the hook (figure 18A) helps disengage the hook barb, so that the quick pull (figure 18B) will jerk the hook free with minimal trauma. Many times a victim has been quoted as asking "When are you going to pull it out?" after the job has been completed.

The dissection method: But at times it just seems we are not to be so lucky and we have to resort to what will probably be a difficult experience for the victim and surgeon alike. This is the case of embedded triple hooks, a hook near the eye, or other situations when the above methods cannot be used. No person in his right mind would attempt this on his own if evacuation to a physician was at all possible. It is tedious, and without a local anesthetic such as injectable lidocaine, extremely painful.

The technique employees the use of either a #11 scalpel blade or an 18 gauge or larger bore hypodermic needle. Examine a hook similar to the one which is embedded in the victim to note the bend in the shank and the location of the barb. You will need to slide the blade along the hook shank, cutting the strands of connective tissue so that the hook can be backed out. If using the needle, you will need to slide it along the hook and attempt to engage the barb, thus shielding connective tissue strands from the barb, allowing the hook to be similarly backed out. This is an elegant method and can result in minimal tissue damage, with only the entry hole left. But it can take time and without local anesthesia the victim would have to be stoic. If available, inject a little 1% lidocaine from the Rx Injectable Kit. Practice using a piece of closed cell foam sleeping pad, rather than human skin, prior to your trip in the bush.

SPLINTER REMOVAL — Prepare the wound with Hibiclens surgical scrub or other solution that does not discolor the skin. Minute splinters are hard enough to see. If the splinter is shallow, or the point buried, use a needle or #11 scalpel blade to tease the tissue over the splinter to remove this top layer. The splinter can then be pried out better.

It is best to be aggressive in removing this top layer and obtaining a substantial bite on the splinter with the splinter forceps (or tweezers), rather than nibbling off the end when making futile attempts to remove with inadequate exposure. When using the splinter forceps, grasp the instrument between the thumb and forefinger, resting the instrument on the middle finger and further resting the entire hand against the victim's skin, if necessary, to prevent tremor. Approach the splinter from the side, if exposed, grasping it as low as possible. Apply triple antibiotic afterwards.

Tetanus immunization should be current within 10 years, or if a dirty wound, within 5 years. If the wound was dirty scrub afterwards with Hibiclens or soapy water. If deep treat as indicated above under PUNCTURE WOUND with hot soaks and antibiotic as indicated.

SUBUNGUAL HEMATOMA — Blood under a fingernail or toenail. Generally caused by a blow to the digit involved, the accumulation of blood under a nail can be very painful. Relieve this pressure by twirling the sharp point of the #11 blade through the nail (using the lightest pressure possible) until a hole is produced and draining effected. Soak in cool water to promote continual drainage of this blood. Treatment for pain with Mobigesic, 1 or 2 tablets every 4 hours or 1 Tylenol #3 every 4 to 6 hours may also be necessary.

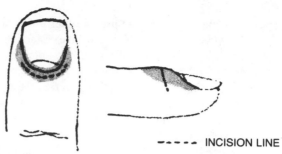

- - - - - INCISION LINE

FIGURE 19. PARONYCHIA

PARONYCHIA — or infection of the nail base. This very painful condition should initially be treated with warm soaks, 15 minutes, every 2 hours, and the use of oral antibiotics such as the doxycycline 100 mg twice daily. Oral pain medication will also be necessary. If the lesion does not respond within 2 days, or if it seems to be getting dramatically worse, an aggressive incision with a #11 blade will be necessary (see figure 19). This wound will bleed freely — allow it to do so. Change bandages as necessary — and continue the soaks and medications as described under ABSCESS.

INGROWN NAIL — This painful infection along the edge of a nail can, at times, be relieved with warm soaks. There are several maneuvers that can hasten healing however. One technique is a taping procedure. A piece of strong tape (such as water-proof tape) is taped to the inflamed skin edge, next to — but not touching — the nail. The tape is fastened tightly to this skin edge with gentle, but firm pressure. By running the tape under the toe, the skin edge can be tugged away from the painful nail and thus relieve the pressure.

Another method is to shave the top of the nail by scraping it with a sharp blade until it is thin enough that it buckles upwards. This "breaks the arch" of the nail and allows the ingrown edge to be forced out of the inflamed groove along the side. The above techniques should be implemented at the first sign of irritation rather than waiting for infection to develop, though even then they are effective. Provide antibiotic such as the doxycycline 100 mg twice daily.

FELON — a deep infection of a finger tip is called a felon. It results in a tense, tender finger pad. Soaking a felon prior to surgery — unlike other infections — does not help and only increases the pain. Treatment is effected by a very aggressive incision, called a fish-mouth incision, made along the tip of the finger from one side to the other and extending deep to the bone! (See figure 20).

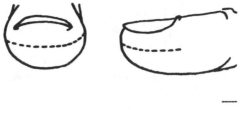

— INCISION LINE

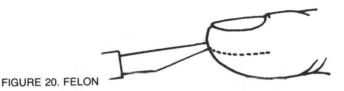

FIGURE 20. FELON

The pain is severe and not helped by local injection of lidocaine. But relief is quick in coming as pressure from the pus build-up is then alleviated. Allow this wound to bleed freely. Soak in warm water for 15 minutes, every 2 hours until drainage ceases (about three days). Give pain medication about one hour prior to your surgical procedure, using the strongest that you have in your kit. Simultaneously start the victim on antibiotic such as the doxycycline 100 mg and repeat twice daily.

SKIN RASH — constitutes a frequent outdoor problem. At times a rash is associated with certain diseases and can help in the diagnosis. If the patient is feverish, or obviously ill, review the sections on lyme disease, Rocky Mountain spotted fever, typhoid fever, syphilis, meningococcemia, strep throat, measles, and mononucleosis. Many infections which cause rash are viral and will not respond to antibiotic. But in the wilderness, with no professional medical help available, rash associated with symptoms of illness can be empirically treated with antibiotic such as the doxycycline 100 mg twice daily for at least 2 days beyond the defervescence (loss of fever). Some of the above infections require longer antibiotic treatment, so it should be continued as indicted if there is a probability that you are dealing with one of them.

Localized rashes without fever are usually due to superficial skin infections, fungal infections or allergic reactions. Itch can be treated with antihistamine or any pain medication. The Non-Rx Oral Medication Unit has Benadryl 25 mg as an antihistamine. One capsule (2 in severe cases) every 6 hours will help with itch from nearly any cause. As itch travels over the same nerves that carry the sensation of pain, any pain medication can also help with itch. Warm soaks generally make itch and rash worse and should be avoided, unless there is evidence of deep infection (see sections on CELLULITIS, ABSCESS above). It is hard to do better than Benadryl with regard to oral antihistamine effect, but it should be noted that Atarax (in the Rx Oral/Topical Unit) and the same medication in injectable form, Vistaril (in the Rx Injectable Unit), also have antihistamine action and can be used for itch.

Cool compresses will sooth a rash. If it is a moist, weeping lesion, wet soaks of dilute epsom salts, boric acid, or even table salt will help dry the lesion (this includes poison ivy). If it is a dry scaly rash, an ointment works the best — much better than a gel, lotion, or cream. Blistered rash are treated best with creams, lotions, or gels. Specific types of rash require specific types of topical medications, however. Also soothing to either a non-weeping lesion or a blistered and weeping lesion is the application of a piece of Spenco 2nd Skin from the Topical Bandaging Unit.

FUNGAL INFECTION — These infections are very slow in spreading, with the lesions becoming larger over a period of weeks to months. They are demarcated by a red and generally raised border and while the skin inside the inflamed area is discolored and itchy, the coloration is not as red as at the border. Fungal infections are found on the feet (tinea pedis — athlete's foot), groin area (*tinea cruris — jock itch*), circular patches on the body (*tinea corporis — ring worm*), and scalp (*tinea capitis* — also called ring worm). From the Non-Rx Topical Bandaging Unit use the miconazole 2% cream. This is currently the best antifungal that can be obtained without a prescription. Apply a thin coat twice daily. Good results should be obtained within 2 weeks for jock itch, but athlete's foot and body ring worm may take 4 weeks. Continue treatment until all evidence of rash is gone, then continue treatment once daily for an additional 3 weeks. If no improvement has been made, you may have the wrong diagnosis or a fungus that is refractory to miconazole.

ALLERGIC DERMATITIS — The hallmark of an allergic dermatitis are vessicles, or small blisters, on red, swollen and very itchy skin. A line of these blisters clinches the diagnosis of allergic, or contact dermatitis. The most common reasons are *poison ivy, poison sumac,* and *poison oak*. Contact with *caterpillars, millipedes* and many plants — even as innocent as various evergreen trees — can induce allergic or toxic skin reactions. A toxic reaction to a noxious substance, such as that from certain insects and plants, is treated the same as an allergic dermatitis. First aid treatment is a thorough cleansing with soap and water. Further treatment is with Benadryl 25 mg every 6 hours from the Non-Rx Oral Medication Unit and twice daily applications of hydrocortisone cream .5% from the Topical Bandaging Unit. Weeping lesions can be treated with wet soaks as mentioned above. An occlusive plastic dressing will allow the rather weak .5% hydrocortisone to work much better.

The Rx Oral/Topical Medication Unit has two very effective medications to treat this problem. Continue use of the Benadryl, but add Decadron 4 mg tablets, one daily for 5 to 7 days and apply the Topicort .25% Ointment in place of the hydrocortisone cream. A thin coat twice daily without an occlusive plastic dressing should work rapidly.

Stinging Nettle causes a severe irritation that can be instantly eliminated by the application of GI jungle juice, which is a 75% mixture of deet insect repellent and 25% isopropyl (rubbing) alcohol. I discovered this neat trick the hard way (accidentally) while camping in fields of the stuff along the Cape Fear River in North Carolina. Since mentioning this in the first edition of Wilderness Medicine in 1979, many others in contact with this plant have confirmed the treatment's instantaneous effectiveness.

SUPERFICIAL SKIN INFECTIONS — Bacterial skin infections generally must be treated with Rx oral antibiotics. A common superficial skin infection is *impetigo*. The normal appearance of this condition is reddish areas around pus filled blisters, which are frequently crusty and scabbed. The lesions spread rapidly over a period of days. The skin is generally not swollen underneath the lesions. A frequent place for it to start is around the nose. It spreads rapidly from scratching and may soon appear anywhere on the body. Early lesions appear as small pimples, which form crusts within 12 to 24 hours. Lesions should be cleaned with surgical soap (or hydrogen peroxide) and then covered with an application of triple antibiotic ointment. Avoid placing bandages on these lesions as the germs can spread under the tape. An oral antibiotic is required for treatment — the ideal being one that can kill resistant staph infections such as Tegopen 250 mg, 4 times daily. The antibiotics in the Rx Oral Kit are not ideal for this, but they should be tried. The Rx Injectable Medication Unit contains Rocephin which would be ideal for this condition. Give 500mg IM once daily. Treatment of *cellulitis* and *abscess* — forms of deep skin infections — are discussed on pages 95 and 96.

POISONING — INGESTION OF POISONOUS PLANTS OR FOOD — The Pittsburgh Poison Control Center manages the vast majority of their poison plant ingestion victims by treatment consisting of vomiting induced by syrup of ipecac. This technique provided totally adequate therapy. 1/2 oz of syrup of ipecac is given orally and two 8 oz glasses of water follow to enhance vomiting. This technique provided superior emptying compared to gastric lavage (stomach pumping) and can even cause the expulsion of particles in the upper portion of the small intestine. If no vomiting occurs, repeat the dose of 1/2 oz of syrup of ipecac in 20 minutes. If all fails, induce vomiting by gagging the throat with a finger or spoon. This latter technique may well be the only method available while in the bush.

POISONING — INGESTION OF PETROLEUM PRODUCTS — The danger from accidentally drinking various pertroleum products, say while siphoning from one container to another, is the danger from accidentally inhaling or aspirating this liquid into the lungs. That will kill. The substances are not toxic enough in the GI tract to warrant the danger of inducing vomiting. Do not worry about swallowing several mouth fulls of any petroleum product. If the person vomits, there is nothing you can do about it, except position them so that there is less chance of aspiration into the lungs — sitting, bending forward is probably ideal. The more volatile the subtance, the more the danger of aspiration. In other words, kerosene is less dangerous than Coleman fuel.

If organic phosphorous pesitcides are dissolved in the fuel, you have a more complex problem. These substances are potentially toxic and must be removed. In the emergency room this would be accomplished by gastric lavage, or stomach pumping. In the bush, if you cannot evacuate the person within 12 hours, you will have to take a chance of inducing vomiting — with possible lethal aspiration — to eliminate the poison. Treat with ipecac as described under poison plant ingestion.

ACUTE JOINT INJURY — Unusual stress across a joint can result in damage to supporting ligaments. Ordinarily this is a temporary stretching damage, but in severe cases rupture of ligaments or even fracture of bones or tears of cartilage can result. These injuries are serious problems and may require surgical repair — this is best done immediately, but can safely be delayed 2 to 3 weeks. Fractures entering the joint space may result in long term joint pain and subsequent arthritis. If not a surgical case, certainly immobilization followed by range of motion physical therapy will be required for an optimum outcome. Cartilage tears do not heal themselves, unlike ligament, tendon, and bone damage. These frequently cause so much future pain and instability that surgical correction is required. Without x-ray and trained medical personnel, how does one approach the acute joint injury in the wilderness?

Proper care of joint injuries must be started immediately. Rest, Ice, Compression, and Elevation form the basis of good first aid management. Cold should be applied for the first 2 days, as continuously as possible. Afterward, applying heat for 20 minutes, 4 times daily is helpful. Cold decreases the circulation, which lessens bleeding and swelling. Heat increases the circulation, which then aids the healing process. This technique applies to all injuries including muscle contusions and bruises.

Elevate the involved joint, if possible. Wrap with elastic bandage or cloth tape to immobilize the joint and provide moderate support once ambulation or use of the joint begins. Take care that the wrappings are not so tightly applied that they cut off the circulation. The Orthopedic Unit of the medical kit has many items that provide safe, yet secure joint support. The Webril orthopedic padding, consisting of long strand non-woven cotton, wrapped around the joint and covered with an elastic bandage is ideal if further swelling is expected. For a very secure wrapping, where no additional swelling is anticipated, use the Unna Boot bandage to provide a more rigid base and over-wrap with the elastic bandage.

Use crutches or other support to take enough weight off an injured ankle and knee to the point that increased pain is not experienced. The patient should not use an injured joint if use causes pain, as this indicates further strain on the already stressed ligaments or fracture. Conversely, if use of the injured part does not cause pain, additional damage is not being done even if there is considerable swelling. If the victim must walk on an injured ankle or knee, and doing so causes considerable pain, then support it the best way possible (wrapping, crutches, decreased carrying load, tight boot for ankle injury) and realize that further damage is being done, but that in your opinion the situation warrants such a sacrifice. Under emergency movement conditions a boot should not be removed from an injured ankle as it may be impossible to replace it. However, one must avoid too much compression of the soft tissue swelling to prevent circulation impairment. Doing additional damage to the ankle and risking circulation damage to the rest of the foot is an important decision to make.

Pain medications may be given as needed, but elevation and decreased use will provide considerable pain relief. See also discussion of fractures on pages 109-111.

DISLOCATIONS — Deformity of a joint after an acute injury can represent bleeding into the joint, fracture near the joint, or dislocation of the joint. Bleeding is usually diffuse and appears as generalized swelling. It may represent significant joint injury and should be treated by splinting in a position of function. Note how an uninjured person holds the joint in question when relaxed. That is the definition of "position of function". For example, the hand is held with the fingers slightly curled when at rest.

Dislocated fingers can generally be reduced by a steady pull (traction) until the joint pops back into place. Injured fingers should be splinted in a position of function, maintaining this slight curl and not splinted straight. The Sam Splint is ideal for this, but it will have to be cut and folded into a proper shape. After splinting for 3 weeks, the injured finger can be "buddy splinted" to the adjacent finger for an additional 2 to 3 weeks which will allow mobilization, yet still provide stability.

One of the more frequent significant injuries is a shoulder dislocation. A shoulder dislocation is a separation of the humerus from the shoulder and is classified as either anterior or posterior. Anterior is by far the most common at a ration of 10:1. Fractures of the head, or top part, of the humerus may be associated with dislocations. In the survival situation during which no evacuation to professional help is feasible, a reduction of the dislocation should be attempted as soon as possible. Muscle spasm and pain will continue to increase the longer the dislocation is allowed to remain untreated.

Anterior dislocations may be identified by comparison to the opposite side. The normal smooth rounded contour of the shoulder, which is convex on the lateral (outside) side, is lost. With anterior displacement the lateral contour is sharply rectangular and the anterior (or front) contour is unusually prominent. The arm is held close to the body and any attempted movement will cause considerable pain.

The best method of reducing the anterior dislocation of the shoulder is the Stimson Maneuver. While other methods exist, this technique puts less force on the shoulder which is particularly important in case fractures of the head of the humerus co-exist with the dislocation. The patient lies face down in the Stimson method on a table or flat, elevated object with the dislocated arm hanging down and the hand hanging free above the floor. Weight is added to the hand to help gentle reduction occur with a minimum of complications, as indicated in Figure 21.

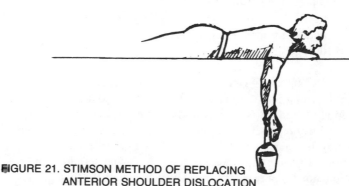

FIGURE 21. STIMSON METHOD OF REPLACING
         ANTERIOR SHOULDER DISLOCATION

Dislocation of the nose is also a common injury. It has been discussed on page 32.

JOINT PAIN — NO ACUTE INJURY — Pain in the joint without history of injury is generally due to an arthritis, bursitis, or tendonitis. Without a history of previous arthritis the latter two become more likely as the actual diagnosis, but the treatment is the same for all three. The most common reason for tendon or joint inflammation is not acute damage, but an over-use injury. The ancient French trapper frequently encountered an Achilles tendonitis while snowshoeing, which they aptly termed "mal de racquette." Persons hammering, chopping wood, or playing tennis are familiar with epicondylitis of the elbow (tennis elbow) which is a tendonitis of the elbow. Tendonitis can occur in the thumb, wrist, in fact any tendon in the body can become inflamed with over-use. Joints similarly become inflamed with repetitive activity or even unusual compression. Cave explorers and canoeists will, on occasion, encounter a patellar bursitis of the knees, and many people have formed bursitis flare-ups in a shoulder due to repeated employment of certain arm actions.

The best medication for chronic joint pain is the Mobigesic from the Non-Rx Oral Medication Unit due to its anti-inflammatory action. One or two tablets every 4 hours will aid in joint pain. Local moist heat application is also helpful. If hot compresses seem to aggravate the pain, switch to a cold compress technique. Avoid making the movements which seem to cause the most pain for 5 to 7 days. Splinting may help during this period. Avoid non-use of the shoulder for longer than 2 weeks as it is prone to adhesion formation and loss of function can result. From the Rx Oral/Topical Medication Unit one could use the Decadron 4 mg, given once daily for 7 days for joint inflammation. The Tylenol #3 may be necessary for pain relief, but it has no anti-inflammation activity.

FRACTURES — Broken bones are a source of much concern when in isolated areas. Each fracture has several critical aspects in its management to consider: 1) loss of circulation or nerve damage if bone spicules are pressing against these structures due to deformity of the fracture; 2) induction of infection if the skin is broken at or near the fracture site; 3) proper alignment of bone fragments so that adequate healing takes place.

At times it will be uncertain whether or not a fracture actually exists. There will be point tenderness, frequently swelling and discoloration over the fracture site or the generalized area, and in obvious cases, deformity and loss of stability. If doubt exists, splint and treat for pain, avoiding the use of the involved part. Within a few days the pain will have diminished and the crisis may be over. If not, the suspicion of fracture will loom even larger.

With proper splinting the pain involved with a fracture will decrease dramatically. Pain medication should be provided as soon as possible. Pain control is discussed on page 17.

The non-Rx Mobigesic or Rx Atarax can be given to aid in muscle spasm control.

Reduction of fractures should be left to the hands of skilled persons — a minimum of common sense, however, can be applied to minimize the damage and to make temporary repairs until a physician can be consulted later. The adage "splint them as they lie" is the golden rule in handling fractures. However, if obvious circulation damage is occurring, namely the pulses distal to the fracture site have ceased, the extremity is turning blue and cold to touch, or numbness is apparent in a portion of the limb distal to the fracture, angulations of the fracture should be straightened to attempt to eliminate the pressure damage. Broken bone edges can be very sharp — in fact a laceration of the blood vessels and nerves may have already occurred, thus causing the above symptoms. An attempt at correcting alignment may cause further damage, thus the recommendation to "split them where they lie". Splints must be well padded to prevent skin damage. Pneumatic splints are available from many outfitters. Fracture splinting is generally well covered in first aid courses. Such a course should be taken prior to any major expedition into the bush. Improvisation is the name of the game in fracture immobilization and having an adequate first aid course provides one with information upon which to improvise. In general, fractures should be splinted in such a manner that the joint above and below the fracture site is immobilized.

HAND FRACTURES can generally be splinted with a cloth rolled in the hand, and the natural grip position of the hand assumed. This grip around the rolled cloth can then be wrapped with gauze to maintain the immobilization. **SHOULDER** injuries should be immobilized with a sling and another band tied around the body to prevent movement. Fractures of the **THIGH** must be immobilized with a padded splint extending beyond the hip, with cloths wrapping the splint around the abdomen as well as the leg. An inner small splint is secured to the medial (inner) portion of the leg. (See *Figure 22*.)

Various traction devices can be improvised to overcome powerful muscle contractions of the thigh which will cause bone ends to override. A commercial device for this purpose is the Thomas splint, available through many medical/surgical suppliers. This device could not be justified except on major climbing expeditions or by rescue teams. Potential

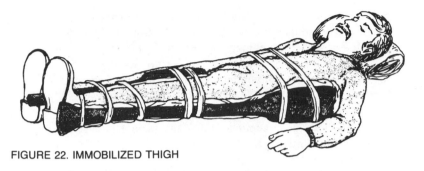

FIGURE 22. IMMOBILIZED THIGH

NECK and BACK injury is a particular reason for taking a first aid course. The management of these injuries can be fraught with disaster. The basic techique is immobilization. (See *Figure 23*).

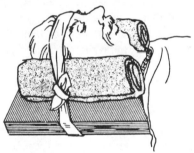

FIGURE 23. IMMOBILIZED HEAD AND NECK

A LACERATION or PUNCTURE WOUND AT THE FRAC-TURE SITE MEANS TROUBLE. Particularly if a spicule of bone is protruding. Wounds of this nature should never be sutured closed, as the incidence of severe infection is then greater. Cleanse the wound thoroughly, hopefully with the Hibiclens surgical scrub. Lacking that, with povidone iodine prep pads, alcohol prep pads, soap and water in decreasing order of effectiveness. Regardless of what is used, do a thorough job of cleansing. This will probably promote bleeding. The aggressiveness of this cleansing action should be done in such a manner as not to cause further damage, but certainly the area must be free of foreign particulate matter and as antiseptic as possible. Cover the wound with triple antibiotic ointment. Protect with sterile gauze dressings, with enough pressure to control bleeding only.

If the patient can be removed to a medical facility within two or three days, leave the bone specules protruding alone — constantly keep the sterile dressing in place and moisten with boiled and cooled water. Spenco 2nd Skin makes an ideal covering for this type of wound. If no such evacuation is possible, after the very thorough cleansing as mentioned above, reduce the fracture with traction on both sides of the break to allow the best alignment possible. Dress wound as mentioned above. In all cases of laceration or puncture wound near a fracture, place the victim on oral antibiotics when available. From the Rx Oral/Topical Medication Unit use the doxycycline 100 mg twice daily. However, if the Rx Injectable Unit is carried, give the Rocephin 1 gm IM daily. This should be continued until the patient is evacuated or the medication runs out.

FRACTURED RIBS — may develop after a blow to the chest. A bad cough or sneeze may also crack ribs! There is point tenderness, exquisite pain with the lightest palpation over the fracture site. The pain at this site will be reproduced by squeezing the rib cage in such a manner as to put a stress across the fracture site. Deep breathing will also produce pain at that location.

It will not be necessary to strap or band the chest, except that such a band might prevent some rib movement and make the patient more comfortable. It is very important for the patient to breath and have some cough reflex to aid in pulmonary hygiene — namely to prevent the accumulation of fluid in the lung which rapidly can lead to a pneumonia. Simply tying a large towel, an undershirt, etc. around the victim's chest should suffice. the fractured rib will take six to eight weeks to heal. A similar pain may be initially present due to a tear of the intercostal muscles or separation of cartilage from the bone of the rib, near the sternum or breat bone. These problems are treated as above. They heal much quicker, generally 3 to 5 weeks.

Treat with pain medication as described on page 17. Avoid unnecessary movement. Treat with an antibiotic if fever starts, such as the doxycycline 100 mg twice daily or the Bactrim DS twice daily as mentioned on page 12.

**BEE STINGS — also Wasp, Yellow Jackets, Hornets (*Hymenoptera* — Stings from these insects hurt instantly and the pain lingers. The danger comes from the fact that some persons are "hypersensitive" to the venom and can have an immediate anaphylactic shock which is life-threatening.

The pain of the sting can be alleviated by almost anything applied topically. Apply cold pack or dibucaine ointment from the Topical/Bandaging Unit. Use oral pain medication such as Mobigesic or stronger Rx medications as necessary. Delayed swelling can be prevented and/or treated with oral antihistamine such as the Benadryl 25 mg taken 4 times daily from the Non-Rx Oral Medication Unit. Immediate swelling, however, can be a sign of impending anaphylaxis and should be more aggressively treated as indicated below.

ANAPHYLACTIC SHOCK — while most common due to insect stings, it may be encountered as a serious allergic reaction to medications, shell fish and other foods, in fact anything to which one has become profoundly allergic. We are not born sensitive to these things, but become allergic with repeated exposures. Those developing anaphylaxis generally have warnings of their severe sensitivity in the form of welts (urticaria) forming all over their body immediately after exposure, the development of an asthmatic attack with respiratory wheezing, or the onset of symptoms of shock.

This deadly form of shock can begin within seconds of exposure. It cannot be treated as indicated in the section on "normal" shock on page 19. The antidote of anaphylactic shock is a Rx drug called epinephrine (Adrenalin). It is available for emergency use as a component of the Anakit (use is described on page 15) or in a special automatic injectable syringe called the EpiPen. I recommend the Anakit as it contains two injections of epinephrine, rather than one and the cost is about half that of the EpiPen. Normal dose is .3 cc for an adult of the 1:1000 epinephrine solution given "subQ" (in the fatty layer beneath the skin). This may have to be repeated in 15 to 20 minutes if the symptoms of wheezing or shock start to return. The Anakit contains a chewable antihistamine which should also be taken immediately, but antihistamines are of no value in treating the shock or asthmatic component of anaphylaxis. If you have oral or injectable Decadron, give a 4 mg tablet or 4 mg injection for protection over the next 12 hours. Anyone experiencing anaphylactic reactions should be evacuated to medical care, even though they have responded to the epinephrine. They are at risk of the condition returning and they should be monitored carefully over the next 24 hours.

SNAKE BITE — The first problem is to determine if the bite was by a poisonous snake and if envenomation took place. If the snake was not seen, you will have to go on symptoms alone — if your powers of identification are feeble, again you must rely on symptoms. The first symptom noted by many is a peculiar tingling in the mouth, often associated with a rubbery or metallic taste. This symptom may develop in minutes and long before any swelling occurs at the bite site. Envenomation may produce instant burning pain. Weakness, sweating, nausea and fainting may occur either with poiscnous snake bites or nonpoisonous bites, simply due to the trauma of being bitten.

Poisonous snakes will generally leave fang marks (but it may be difficult to identify two perfect fang marks which are supposed to be so characteristic of the pit vipers — the coral snake will not have fang marks, but will chew the victim and induce venom into the macerated tissue). With envenomation, within one hour there will generally be swelling, pain, tingling and/or numbness at the bite site. As several hours pass, ecchymosis (bruising) and discoloration of the skin begins and becomes progressively worse. Vesicles may form, sometimes the blisters are filled with blood. The superficial blood vessels may form clots or become thrombosed. This, in turn, could lead to sloughing and necrosis in several days. Chills and fever may begin, followed by muscle tremor, decrease in blood pressure, headache, blurred vision and bulging eyes.

With regard to the visual identification of the most common poisonous snakes in North America — the Pit Vipers (Family Crotalidae) (rattlesnakes, copperheads and water moccasins), take their names from the deep pit between the eye and nostril, which is a heat-receptor organ. Most of them have a triangular head and they have a cat-like verticle elliptical pupil. Coral snakes (Micruruns fulvius) (Family Elapidae), while not pit vipers, also have the verticle elliptical pupils. Some nonpoisonous snakes do also. Color variation in coral snakes makes the old saying that if the "yellow is separated from the black, it is nonpoisonous" (i.e. not a coral snake, but a king snake, etc.), a very treacherous method of identification.

TREATMENT OF SNAKE BITE — NONPOISONOUS SNAKE — Get away from the snake. Cleanse the bitten area with surgical scrub — apply suction with the Extractor to promote evacuation of puncture debris. No constriction band should be used. Treat as under puncture wound on page 97. The victim should have had a tetanus shot within 5 years.

PIT VIPER BITE — Not everyone bitten by a pit viper will have envenomation injury — fully 20% of rattlesnake and 30% of cotton mouth water moccasin and copperhead bites will not envenomate during their bite. DO NOT APPLY COLD — this is associated with increased tissue damage. 1) Immobilize the injured part at heart level or slightly above in a position of function. 2) Apply an elastic bandage with a firm wrap from the bite site towards the body, leaving the bite exposed if you have an Extractor for further treatment, covered if you do not. 3) Apply suction with the Extractor. Making incisions actually decreases the amount of venom that can be removed with this device. If applied within 3 minutes as much as 35% of the venom may be removed with the Extractor. After 1/2 hour, less than 3% more will be removed so further suction can be terminated. 4) Treat for shock (page 19) and evacuate to professional medical help.

The Extractor has simplified the field care of snake bite due to its high amount of vacuum and effectiveness. It must be carried by anyone entering an area with poisonous snakes. If you do not have an extractor, then you must decide on whether or not to use incision and low grade suction (mouth or suction cups). This technique will work, but it is associated with additional trauma, possible wound infection, danger to the first aider (when using mouth suction), increased chance of shock, and questionable medical-legal complications later. A rule of thumb: if evacuation to qualified medical help cannot be made within 1-1/2 hours, then incision and suction is justified with a pit viper bite. The decision to perform this must be made within the first several minutes as various studies have shown a similar effectiveness rate to the Extractor results discussed above, with the results becoming nil within 1/2 hour. Make a shallow incision of about 1/8 inch deep and 1/2 inch long through the identified fang marks, connecting them if possible with one incision. Use common sense and do not cut underlying structures such as obvious blood vessels at the surface, tendons, etc. Never cut an "X" as cruciate incisions make ugly wounds that do not heal well.

Steroids should not be used routinely in poison snake bites. Other than the use of antivenin, treat as indicated under puncture wound on page 97.

Antivenin: Wyeth produces a polyvalent Crotalidae antivenin, which comes in a freeze-dried form, complete with a bottle of diluent and syringe assembly. This may be stored for fairly long periods at room temperature.

Each kit has a small bottle of horse serum to skin test the potential recipient, as the antivenin is made from horse serum. Many people are highly sensitive to the horse serum and it is possible that for these people this antivenin preparation may be more lethal than the snake bite. The test dose of the horse serum must be kept refrigerated. It would seem that members of an expedition heading into potential poisonous snake-infested areas could ideally be tested for sensitivity to the horse serum prior to departure. This would then allow the administration to be made without waiting 15 minutes for a skin test. It would also allow the non-refrigerated transport of the antivenin sets. However, this is dangerous as even skin testing can cause sensitization to develop in the individual and may result in anaphylactic shock upon giving the supposedly safe antivenin. I mention this idea simply to warn against trying it. However, a physician can order a special test called a Radioallergosorbent Test (RAST) that can determine probable sensitivity to horse serum without exposure to it. The use of the antivenin, and the quantities to be given are described in the brochure that comes with each ampule.

Generally, the minimal amount for an adult would be 3 amps, for a child 5 amps. For a swollen hand 5 to 8 amps IV initially, with another 8 ready to go if the swelling progresses. Severe envenomation may require over 38 amps! This antivenin is only available by prescription and the current wholesale drug cost is $40. Approximately 7 to 10 days later, recipients of so much horse serum will develop a delayed reaction called "serum sickness." This will generally have to be treated with antihistamines (such as Benadryl) and steroids (such as Decadron).

CORAL SNAKE BITE — The envenomation by this snake is via a slow chewing process, so that rapid withdrawal from the attack may have resulted in no uptake of venom by the victim. For treatment: 1) Treat for shock as necessary; 2) Wash the bitten area promptly; 3) Apply suction with the Extractor; 4) Avoid incisions; 5) Apply an elastic bandage with a firm wrap from the bite site towards the body, leaving the bite exposed if you have an Extractor for further treatment, covered if you do not; 6) Treat as a puncture wound and note tetanus precautions (page 97 and Appendix A).

Since the Coral Snake is an elapid, like the cobra, signs and symptoms of envenomation take time to develop and deterioration then proceeds so rapidly that the antidote may be of no avail. Many experts feel the antidote should be given immediately after skin testing in all cases. Most authorities feel 2 units of the Wyeth Micruris fulvis antivenin should be given IV immediately. Some would use 10 amps of the antivenin. Note the discussion below under cobra bites.

COBRA, RUSSELL'S VIPER, GREEN MAMBA, KRAIT BITES — Most areas of the world have a local source of antivenin for the species of snakes that are of concern in that locale. In Africa many of the antivenins come from the Union of South Africa, but trade is greatly restricted to many other African countries. The use of a class of compounds called anticholinesterases can be life-saving when dealing with neurotoxic envenomation, particularly if the antivenin is not available. A suggested protocol is the administration of .6 mg of atropine IV (.05 mg/kg for children) to control intestinal cramping followed by 10 mg of Tensilon (.25 mg/kg for children). If there is improvement, further control of symptoms can be obtained by titration of a dose of neostigmine .025 mg/kg/hr by IV injection or continuous infusion. I have provided this recent information for the benefit of a physician member of a party that might be at risk, although the medications are not included in the recommended Rx Injectable Unit.

SPIDER BITES — Generally spiders will make a solitary bite, rather than several. If the person awakens with multiple bites, he has collided with some other arthropod most likely.

BLACK WIDOW — (Latrodectus mactans) Generally a glossy black with a red hourglass mark on the abdomen. Sometimes the hourglass mark is merely a red dot or the two parts of the hourglass do not connect. At times the coat is not shiny and it may contain white. The bite may be only a pin-prick, but generally a dull cramping pain begins within one quarter of an hour and this may spread gradually until it involves the entire body. The muscles may go into spasms and the abdomen becomes board-like. Extreme restlessness is typical. The pain can be excruciating. Nausea, vomiting, swelling of eyelids, weakness, anxiety (naturally), pain on breathing may all develop. A healthy adult can usually survive, with the pain abating within several hours and the remaining symptoms disappearing in several days.

An ice cube on the bite, if available, may reduce local pain. A specific antidote is available (*L. mactans* antivenim from Merck, Sharp, & Dohme) which should be given after skin testing to persons under 16 and over 65, heart or kidney patients, or those with very severe symptoms. The dose is one vial diluted in 15 to 50 ml of saline and given IV over ten minutes. A specific treatment for relieving muscle spasm is methocarbamol (Robaxin) 100 mg given as a bolus into an IV line at 1 ml/min. After the initial bolus, a constant infusion of 200 mg/hr IV or 500 mg by mouth every 6 hours can be used. This medication has not been included in the Wilderness Medical Kit, but adequate pain relief can be sought by using the Mobigesic from the Non-Rx Oral Unit, the Tylenol #3 and Atarax from the Rx Oral/Topical Unit, or the Nubain and Vistaril from the Rx Injectable Medication Unit.

BROWN RECLUSE — (Loxosceles reclusa and related species) A brown coat with a black violin marking on the cephalothorax or top part of the spider; the initial bite is mild and may be overlooked at the time. In an hour or two, a slight redness may appear; by several hours a small bleb appears at the bite site. At times the wound begins to appear as a bull's eye with several rings of red and blanched circles around the bite. The bleb ruptures, forming a crust, which then sloughs off; a large necrotic ulcer forms which gradually enlarges. Over the first 36 hours, vomiting, fever, skin rash and joint pain may develop — and hemolysis of blood may be massive.

Apply ice to the wound as soon as possible. An antivenin has been developed from rabbits and is being used experimentally. Dapson 100 mg twice daily (a medication used in the treatment of leprosy) has been beneficial. Dapson is effective during the early stages of treatment as it works on decreasing the severity of the inflammation caused by the bite toxin. Prophylactic use of antibiotic has been recommended. Avoid the application of heat to this wound, even though it is inflamed and necrotic. Early excision of the bite was recommended as the standard of care of this bite, but treatment with antivenin and Dapson negates the necessity of this approach. Without their availability, early diagnosis is important since many of the above symptoms can be alleviated if the bitten area is literally excised, or cut out. This should be performed during the first 8 hours, ideally by a physician — if the diagnosis is certain. Excision should be performed when the necrotic area has grown to .4 inch (1 cm) in size and should extend to include the red, indurated surrounding tissue. From the Rx Oral/Topical Unit give Decadron 4 mg every 6 hours (your medical kit supply will be exhausted in 2 1/2 days, but it is doubtful that steroid therapy is of benefit after that time). Apply triple antibiotic ointment from the topical bandaging unit and cover with Spenco 2nd Skin dressing.

CATERPILLAR REACTIONS — The puss caterpillar (*Megalopyge opercularis*) of the southern US and the gypsy moth caterpillar (*Lymantria dispar*) of the northeastern US have bristles that cause an almost immediate skin rash and welt formation. Treatment includes patting the victim with a piece of adhesive tape to remove these bristles. Further treatment is discussed on page 104.

MILLIPEDE REACTIONS — Millipedes do not bite, but contact can cause skin irritation. Cold packs can reduce discomfort. Wash thoroughly and treat as indicated on page 104.

CENTIPEDE BITES — Some of the larger centipedes can inflict a painful bite that causes a local swelling and painful, red lesion. Treatment with a cold pack is usually sufficient. Some bites are severe and regional lymph node enlargement may occur, which will be a swelling of the nodes generally at the joints along the blood flow pattern towards the heart from the bite site. Swelling at the bite location may persist for weeks. Adequate treatment consists of pain medication and local application of dibucaine ointment. Infiltration of the area with lidocaine 1% from the Rx Injectable Unit provides instant relief and is justified in severe cases.

MOSQUITO BITES — To prevent bites use a DEET (n,n diethyl-m-toluamide) product of 12% or greater. The ideal strength in my opinion is a 75% mixture of deet in 25% rubbing alcohol. This can be made by cutting Muskol or other 100% deet brand. The application is smoother, less expensive, and equally effective. Adequate mosquito netting for the head and for the tent or cot while sleeping is essential. I have not found Vitamin B1 (thiamine) to be an effective preventative oral agent, but the recommended dose by those who do is 100 mg daily for 1 week prior to departure and daily thereafter. Electronic sound devices to repel these critters have never dented mosquito buzzing or biting enthusiasm in the far north in my experience, but I have friends who use them enthusiastically (under less obnoxious circumstances).

A considerable number of bites, or sensitivity to bites, may require an antihistamine, such as Benadryl 25 mg capsules every 6 hours from the Non-Rx Oral Medication Unit. Dibucaine ointment 1% from the Topical Bandaging Unit, applied every 6 hours, can provide local itch relief.

BLACKFLIES — A remarkable repellent is Skin So Soft marketed by your local Avon lady. It is sold as a bath oil, but direct application works better for protection from black flies than 100% DEET. DEET compounds will work, but concentration must be 30% or greater and even the pure formula will work only a short time. A DEET repellent may be applied over Skin So Soft when combating both black flies and mosquitos. Netting and heavy clothes that can be sealed at the cuffs may be required. All black fly species like to land and crawl, worming their way under and through protective clothing and netting. They can cause nasty sores which are usually self-limited, although at times slow healing. If infection is obvious, treat as indicated in the section on skin infection on page 95. Dibucaine ointment 1% will provide local pain relief. Benadryl 25 mg every 6 hours will help reduce swelling and itch.

NO-SEE-UMS, AND BITING GNATS — The scourge of the North Country, or any country in which they may be found. Many local people refer to any small black fly as a "No-See-Um", but the true bug by that name is indeed very hard to see. They usually come out on a hot, sticky night. The attack is sudden and feels like fire over your entire exposed body surface area. Under the careful examination of a flashlight, you will notice an incredibly small gnat struggling with his head down, merrily chomping away. Make the bug portion of the previous sentence plural please. This is an ideal time for application of the Avon Skin So Soft to prevent these bites. A strong DEET product of 30% or greater will also help. Immersion in cold water will help temporarily. One remedy for the sting which I understand works quite well, but which I have never had along to try, is an application of Absorbine Jr!

Gnats on the other hand are a small black fly whose bite is seldom felt. But these gentle biters leave behind a red pimple-like lesion to remind you of their visit. A rash of these pimples around the neck and ankles attests to their ability to sneak through protective clothing. Treat severe cases with Benadryl 25 mg every 6 hours. Application of the 1% dibucaine ointment provides local relief.

SCORPION STING — Most North American scorpion stings are relatively harmless. Stings usually cause only localized pain and slight swelling. The wound may feel numb. Benadryl and Mobigesic may be all that is required for treatment. A cold pack will help relieve local pain.

The potentially lethal *Centruroides sculptuatus* is the exception to this rule. This yellow colored scorpion lives in Mexico, New Mexico, Arizona, and the California side of the Colorado River. The sting causes immediate, severe pain with swelling and subsequent numbness. The neurotoxin injected with this bite may cause respiratory failure. Respiratory assistance may be required (see page 49). Tapping on the wound lightly with your finger will cause the patient to withdraw due to severe pain. This is an unusual reaction and does not occur with most insect stings. A specific antivenin is available in Mexico and is also produced by the Poisonous Animals Laboratory at Arizona State University for local use. In addition to the antivenin, atropine may be needed to reduce muscle cramping, blurred vision, hypertension, respiratory difficulty, and excessive salivation. This is not included in the Wilderness Medical Kit. Methocarbamol may be given as described in the section on Black Widow Spider bites (page 117). Narcotics such as Demerol and morphine can increase the toxicity and should be avoided. Mobigesic from the Non-Rx Oral Medical Unit may be given.

ANT, FIRE ANT — The latter can produce an intensely painful bite. While holding on tightly with his pincer and pivoting around, the ant then stings repeatedly in as many places as the stinger can reach, causing a cluster of small, painful blisters to appear. These can take 8 to 10 days to heal. Treatment is with cold packs and pain medication. Large local reactions may require antihistamine such as the Benadryl 25 mg, 2 capsules every 6 hours and even Decadron 4 mg once daily. Local application of dibucaine ointment 1% can provide some relief. Treat with pain medication as required.

The greatest danger is to the hypersensitive individual who may have an anaphylactic reaction. This should be treated as indicated under ANAPHYLACTIC SHOCK, page 113.

CATFISH STINGS — Apply hot water as indicated under STING RAY. The wound must be properly cleaned and irrigated using surgical scrub, if available, or soap. Place the patient on oral antibiotic for several days to decrease the chance of wound infection which is common with this injury. Treat infected wound as described on page 95.

SEA URCHIN — Punctures from sea urchin spines cause severe pain and burning. Besides trauma from the sharp spines, some species inject a venom. The wound can appear red and swollen or even blue to black from a harmless dye which may be contained in the spines. Generalized symptoms are rare, but may include weakness, numbness, muscle cramps, nausea, and occasionally shortness of breath. The spines should be removed thoroughly — a very tedious process. Very thin spines may be absorbed by the body without harm, but some may form a reactive tissue around them (granulomas) several months later. Spines may migrate into joints and cause pain and inhibit movement or lodge against a nerve and cause extreme pain. The discoloration of the dye causes no problems, but may be mistaken for a thin spine. Relief may be obtained by soaking in hot water (110 to 113 F) for 20 to 30 minutes. Vinegar or acetic acid soaks several times a day may help dissolve spines that are not found. Evacuation and treatment by a physician is advisable.

JELLYFISH — Tentacles can cause mild pricking to burning, shooting, terrible pain. The worse danger is shock and drowning. Avoid the use of hot water in treating this injury. First, pour ocean water over the injury. Try to remove the tentacles with gloved hands. Pour alcohol (or ideally formalin) over the wound, which will prevent the nematocysts from firing more poison. Both ammonia or vinegar would work, but not as well as formalin or alcohol. Urine may be used, but do not use fresh water. Powder the area with a dry powder such as flour or baking powder. Gently scrape off the mess with a knife, clam shell or other sharp instrument, but avoid cutting the nematocysts with a sharp blade. Apply hydrocortisone cream .5% 4 times daily from the Topical Bandaging Unit or Topicort .25% twice daily from the Rx Oral/Topical Unit for inflammation.

CORAL STINGS — These injuries are treated as indicated under JELLYFISH.

CORAL CUTS, BARNACLE CUTS — Clean the wound thoroughly — trivial wounds can later flare into real disasters that may go on for years. Scour thoroughly with a coarse cloth or soft brush and surgical scrub or soapy water. Then apply hydrogen peroxide to help bubble out fine particles and bacteria. Apply triple antibiotic ointment from the Topical Bandaging Unit. Manage this wound as discussed in the section on laceration care, page 88. If an infection ensues, treat as indicated on page 95.

STING RAY — The damage is done by the barbed tail, which lacerates the skin, imbedding pieces of tail material and venom into the wound. The wound bleeds heavily, pain increases over 90 minutes and takes 6 to 48 hours to abate.

Immediately rinse the wound with sea water and remove any particles of the tail sheath which are visible as these particles continue to release venom. Hot water is the treatment of choice — applied as soon as possible and as hot as the patient can stand it (110 — 113 F). The heat will destroy the toxin rapidly and remove the pain that the patient is experiencing. After hot water has been applied and all tail particles removed, the wound may be closed with taping techniques (see page 90). Elevation of the wound is important. If particularly dirty, leave the wound open and continue to use intermittent hot soaks as described on page 95. Questionably dirty wounds should be treated with Bactrim DS 1 tablet twice daily or doxycycline 100 mg twice daily from the Rx Oral Medication Unit. As these are nasty, painful wounds, treat for shock from the onset.

SCORPION FISH — Same treatment as STING RAY.

SPONGE RASH — Sponges handled directly from the ocean can cause an allergic reaction that appears immediately. Fine spicules may also break off in the outer layer of skin also causing inflammation. It will be difficult to tell whether your victim is suffering from the allergic reaction or the spicules, or both. Soak the affected skin by applying vinegar to a cloth and covering for 15 minutes. Dry the skin and pat with the adhesive side of tape to remove sponge spicules. Again soak in vinegar for 5 minutes. An application of rubbing alcohol for 1 minute has been suggested. Then apply hydrocortisone cream .5% four times a day from the Non-Rx Topical Bandaging Unit or Topicort .25% twice daily from the Rx Oral/Topical Medication Unit for several days until the inflammation subsides.

TYPHOID FEVER — This disease is characterized by headache, chills, loss of appetite, back ache, constipation, nosebleed, and tenderness of the abdomen to palpation. The temperature rises daily for 7 to 10 days. The fever is maintained at a high level for 7 to 19 more days, then drops over the next 10 days. The pulse rate is low for the amount of fever (generally, the pulse rate will increase 10 beats per minute for every one degree of temperature elevation over normal for that individual) With typhoid fever, a pulse rate of 84 may occur with a temperature of 104 degrees farenheit. Between the 7th and 10th day of illness, rose-colored splotches — which blanche when pressure is applied — appear in 10% of patients. The drug of choice for this illness is chloramphenicol, which is a very treacherous drug to use. If an expedition is heading to Mexico or Southeast Asia, it would be best to avoid dependence upon chloramphenicol, as a number of resistant strains have been isolated in these areas. IV Ampicillin (6 grams per day) is the drug of choice in these areas, but an oral medication useful as a back-up drug for penicillin sensitive individuals is Bactrim DS from the Rx Oral Medication Unit, 1 tablet 3 times a day. Diarrhea may become important in the latter stages of this illness. Replacement of fluids is especially important during the phases of high fever. Patients with relapses should be given another 5-day course of the Bactrim. Immunization prior to departure to endemic areas is useful in curtailing the severity of this infection (see Appendix A).

COLORADO TICK FEVER — A viral disease spread by Ixodid (hard-shelled) ticks, this disease is 20 times more common than Rocky Mountain Spotted Fever in Colorado. It is also found in the other states of the Western Rocky Mountains and provinces of Western Canada. It is most frequent in April-May at low altitudes and June-July at high altitudes. Onset is abrupt, with chills, fever of 100.4 degrees to 104 degrees, muscle ache, headache, eye pain, and eye sensitivity to light (photophobia). The patient feels weak and nauseated, but vomiting is unusual. During the first 2 days, up to 12% of victims develop a rash. In half the cases, the fever disappears after 2 to 3 days and the patient feels well for 2 days. Then a second bout of illness starts which lasts intensely for 2 to 4 days. This second phase subsides with the patient feeling weak for 1 to 2 additional weeks. This disease requires no treatment other than bed rest, fluids to prevent dehydration, and medications to treat fever and aches. However, as the same ticks can also spread potentially dangerous Rocky Mountain Spotted Fever, treatment with doxycycline (100 mg twice daily) as described in that section should be started immediately and this therapy continued for 14 days. This should be accomplished without waiting for the characteristic rash of Rocky Mountain Spotted Fever or the fever pattern of Colorado Tick Fever to develop or for a firm diagnoses of either to be established by a physician.

TRICHINOSIS — is caused by eating improperly cooked meat infected with the cysts of this parasite. It is most common in pigs, bears (particularly Polar bears) and some marine mammals. Nausea and diarrhea or intestinal cramping may appear within 1 to 2 days, but it generally takes 7 days after indigestion. Swelling of the eyelids is very characteristic on the 11th day. Afterwards, muscle soreness, fever, pain in the eyes and subconjunctival hemorrhage (see page 29) develop. If If enough contaminated food is ingested this can be a fatal disease. Most symptoms disappear in 3 months. Treatment is with pain medication (Mobigesic from the Non-Rx Oral Medication Unit or Tylenol #3 from the Rx Oral Medication Unit). The use of steroids such as Decadron (20 mg/day for 3 or 4 days, followed by reduced dosage over the next 10 days) is indicated in severe cases. Thiabendazole is a specific drug for use in this condition, given orally in doses of 25 mg/kg of body weight twice daily for 5 to 10 days. The best prevention is cooking suspected meat at 150 degrees farenheit for 30 minutes for each pound of meat.

ROCKY MOUNTAIN SPOTTED FEVER — This is an acute and serious infection caused by a microorganism called *Rickettsia rickettsii* and transmitted by *Ixodid* (hard-shelled) ticks. It is most common in the states of North Carolina, Virginia, Maryland, the Rocky Mountain States, and the state of Washington. The peak incidence of cases is from May to September. Onset of infection is abrupt, after a 3 to 12-day incubation period (average 7 days from the tick bite). Fever reaches 103 degrees to 104 degrees farenheit within two days. There is considerable headache, chills, and muscle pain at the onset. In four days a rash appears on wrists, ankles, soles, palms, and then spreads to the trunk. Initially pink, this rash turns to dark blotches and even ulcers in severe cases. Any suspected case of Rocky Mountain Spotted Fever should be considered a MEDICAL EMERGENCY. Do not wait for the rash to develop, rather start the patient on the antibiotic from the Rx medical kit. Give doxycycline 100 mg, 1 tablet every 12 hours and keep on this dosage schedule until the total time from the onset of the disease is 14 days. This is a drug of choice and its early use can cut the death rate from 20% to nearly zero. Do not wait for the rash to appear or a firm diagnoses to be made. The sooner the antibiotic is used, the greater the chance for total recovery. Prevention is by the careful removal of ticks, the use of insect repellent and protective clothing.

(Rabbit Fever; Deer Fly Fever) TULAREMIA — This disease can be contracted through exposure to ticks, deer flies, or mosquitos. It is also possible to have cuts infected when working with the pelts, or eating improperly cooked infected rabbits. Similarly, muskrats, foxes, squirrels, mice and rats can spread the disease via direct contact with the carcasses. Stream water may become contaminated by these animals. An ulcer appears when a wound is involved and lymph nodes become enlarged first in nearby areas and then throughout the body. Pneumonia normally develops. The disease lasts 4 weeks in untreated cases. Mortality in treated cases is almost zero, while in untreated cases it ranges from 6% to 30%. Treatment of choice is streptomycin, but doxycycline suggested for the Rx Oral/Topical Medical Unit works extremely well. The average adult would require an initial dose of 2 tablets, followed by 1 tablet every 12 hours. Continue therapy for 5 to 7 days after the fever has been broken.

ENCEPHALITIS — Encephalitis from Group A Arbovirus (Western Equine Encephalitis, Eastern Equine Encephalitis, Venezuelan Equine Encephalitis) in Alaska, U.S., and Canada, and Group B Arbovirus (St. Louis Encephalitis) in the U.S. can be prevented by liberal use of repellent and covering exposed areas with netting or clothing to prevent bites from infected mosquitos. Symptoms of these illnesses include high fever (104 degrees farenheit) and generally headache, stiff neck and vomiting and, at times, diarrhea. These cases can be fatal and require evacuation to medical help. Cool the patient with external means (cool water, fanning), and the use of aspirin or Mobigesic. The disease occurs in epidemics; be very careful of mosquito exposure when the disease becomes prevalent.

SCHISTOSOMIASIS (Bilharziasis, Blood Flukes, Safari Fever) — Blood trematodes or flukes are responsible for this disease. The eggs are deposited in fresh water and hatch into motile miracidia which infect snails. After development in the snails, active cercariae emerge which penetrate exposed human skin. Swimming, wading, or drinking fresh water must be avoided in infected areas.

Schistosoma mansoni is found in tropical Africa, part of Venezuela, several Caribbean islands, the Guianas, Brazil and the Middle East. *S. japonicum* is encountered in China, Japan, the Philippines, and Southeast Asia. *S. haematobium* is in Africa, the Middle East, and small portions of India and islands in the Indian Ocean. The former two species are excreted in the stools and the latter in urine. Shedding may occur for years. No isolation is required of patients. Specific treatments for the various species are available. Check for latest information on dangerous areas by contacting Herchmer Medical Group for specific country update or International Medical Assistance for Travellers (see Appendix A).

Initial penetration of the skin causes a itchy rash. After entry, the organism enters the blood stream, migrates through the lungs, and eventually lodges in the blood vessels draining either the gut or the bladder, depending upon the species. While the worms are maturing the victim will have fever, lethargy, cough, rash, abdominal pain, and frequently nausea. In acute infections caused by *S. mansoni* and *S. japonicum*, victims develop a mucoid, bloody diarrhea and tender liver enlargement. Chronic infection leads to fibrosis of the liver with distention of the abdomen. In *S. haematobium* infections the bladder becomes inflamed and eventually fibrotic. Symptoms include painful urination, urgency, blood in urine, and pelvic pain.

CHAGA'S DISEASE (AMERICAN TRYPANOSOMIASIS) —

The disease caused by *Trypanosoma cruzi*, a protozoan hemoflagellate, is transmitted through the feces of a brown insect called the "kissing bug" or "assassin bug" in North American. This bug is a member of the *Reduviidae* family. A name popular in South America is "vinchuca" derived from a word which means "one who lets himself fall down." These bugs live in palm trees, thatching in native huts, and like to drop on their victims while sleeping, frequently biting them on the face or exposed arms. Bitten patients rub the feces into the bite site, thus causing the innoculaton of the infectious agent.

This disease is located in parts of South and Central America. Check for latest information on dangerous areas by contacting Herchmer Medical Group for specific country update or International Medical Assistance for Travellers (see Appendix A).

At first this disease may have no symptoms. A "chagoma" or red nodule develops at the site of the original infection. This area may then lose its pigmentation. After 1 to 2 weeks, a firm swelling of one eyelid occurs, known as Ramoana's sign. The swelling becomes purplish in color, lymph node swelling in front of the ear on the same side may occur. In a few days a fever develops, with generalized lymph node swelling. Rapid heart rate, spleen and liver enlargement, swelling of the legs, and meningitis or encephalitis may occur. Serious conditions also can include acute heart failure. In most cases, however, the illness subsides in about 3 months and the patient appears to be living a normal life. The disease continues, however, slowly destroying the heart until 10 to 20 years later chronic congestive heart failure becomes apparent. The underlying cause may never be known, especially in a traveler who has left the endemic area. In some areas of Brazil, the disease attacks the colon, causing flaccid enlargement with profound constipation. This disease is a leading cause of death in South America, generally due to heart failure. As many as 15 million people in South America may be infected. Special blood test are available through State Boards of Health and Centers for Disease Control. Supportive treatment is given during acute disease and specific treatments are being developed.

AFRICAN SLEEPING SICKNESS (AFRICAN TRYPANO-SOMIASIS) — Two species of trypanosomes cause this disease which is transmitted by the bite of the tsetse fly. The severity of the disease depends upon the species encountered.

The infection is confined to the area of Africa between 15 degrees north and 20 degrees south of the equator — the exact distribution of the tsetse fly. Man is the only reservoir of *T. gambiense* found in West and Central Africa, while wild game is the principle reservoir of *T. rhodesiense* of East Africa.

T. gambiense infection starts with a nodule or a chancre that appears briefly at the site of a tsetse fly bite. Generalized illness appears months to years later and is characterized by lymph node enlargement at the back of the neck and intermittent fever. Months to years after this development invasion of the central nervous system may occur, noted by behavioral changes, headache, loss of appetite, back ache, hallicinations, delusions, and sleeping. In *T. rhodesiense* infection the generalized illness begins 5 to 14 days after the nodule or chancre develops. It is much more intense than the gambian variety and may include acute central nervous system and cardiac symptoms, fever, and rapid weight loss. It has a high rate of mortality. If untreated, death usually occurs within one year.

CHOLERA — This intestinal infection is caused by a bacterium *Vibrio cholerae* which produces profuse, painful diarrhea. Death can come from dehydration, indeed the death toll can reach the tens of thousands during an epidemic. Ingestion of water contaminated with the bacterium causes spread of the disease. Man is the only documented host for this disease.

In the past 20 years cholera has spread from India and Southeast Asia to Africa, the Middle East, and Southern Europe. A vaccine for prevention is available and is required for entry into some counties. Check for latest information on active disease areas and countries requiring immunization for entry by contacting Herchmer Medical Group for specific country update or International Medical Assistance for Travellers (see Appendix A).

Treatment is with oral rehydration as indicated on page 78. The antibiotic of choice is doxycycline 100 mg twice daily or the alternate drug is Bactrim DS twice daily, both in the Rx Oral Medication Unit. Tylenol #3 can be used for symptomatic relief, 1 tablet every 4 hours for cramping and diarrhea (see page 78).

DENGUE, BREAKBONE FEVER, DANDY FEVER — This viral infection is caused by a virus (Group B arbovirus or flavivirus) and is spread by bites from *Aedes aegypti* mosquito.

Dengue is endemic throughout the tropics and subtropics. Check for latest information on active disease areas and countries receptive to this disease by contacting Herchmer Medical Group for specific country update.

After an incubation period of 3 to 15 (usually 5 to 8) days, there is a sudden onset of fever (104 F), chills, headache, low back ache, pain behind the eyes with movement of the eyes, extreme aching in the legs and joints. The eyes are red and a transient flushing or pale pink rash occurs, mostly on the face. There is a relatively slow pulse rate for the temperature (see page 15). The fever lasts 48 to 96 hours, followed by 24 hours of no fever and a sense of well being. A second rapid temperature increase occurs, but generally not as high as the first. A bright rash spreads from the arms/legs to the trunk, but generally not the face. Palms and soles may be bright red and swollen. There is a severe headache and other body aches as well. The fever, rash, and headache constitute the "dengue triad." The illness lasts for weeks, but mortality is nil. Treatment is rest and the use of pain and fever medication. A condition called Dengue Hemorrhagic Fever Shock Syndrome is lethal and occurs in patients younger than 10 exclusively; generally infants under 1 year of age. Dengue may be confused with Colorado tick fever, typhus, yellow fever, or other hemorrhagic fevers.

MALARIA — Human malaria is caused by four species of protozoan: *Plasmodium falciparum, P. vivax, P. ovale,* and *P. malariae.* The infection is acquired from the bite of an infected female Anopheles mosquito. It may also be spread by blood transfusion. Falciparum malaria is the most serious — while all forms of this disease make people ill and may be lethal, this is the one that kills.

Regions of the world where malaria may be acquired are sub-Saharan Africa, parts of Mexico and Central America, Haiti, parts of South America, the Middle East, the Indian subcontinent and Southeast Asia. The mainstay of *P. falciparum* prevention has been chloroquine (Aralen) 500 mg, 1 tablet every week starting one week before departure, continuing during the trip, and for 6 weeks after returning. Resistance to chloroquine by the deadly *P. falciparum* has become widespread. For travelers in resistant areas contemplating trips of greater than 3 weeks duration, the drug Fansidar (pyrimethamine-sulfadoxine), 1 tablet each week should be taken along with the weekly dose of chloroquine. Persons with a sulfa allergy may not take this drug. Persons developing a rash or any skin problem while on Fansidar must cease taking it immediately, as a fatal reaction may occur. If a trip is of short duration (less than 3 weeks) in a chloroquine resistant area, the traveler should take the usual dose of chloroquine and carry a three tablet dose of Fansidar for consumption at one time as a presumptive treatment in case the symptoms of malaria develop (ache, fever, or any questionable flu-like symptoms). This person should also seek medical help as soon as possible. An alternate drug regimen, especially necessary when *P. falciparum* become resistant to both chloroquine and Fansidar, is the use of doxycycline 100 mg to be taken once daily for prevention.

In areas with relapsing malaria (*P. vivax* and *P. ovale*), primaquine should be taken 1 tablet daily during the last 2 weeks of chloroquine therapy. This is usually appropriate for those with long exposure in areas with a high concentration of these strains of malaria. The Herchmer data base (see Appendix A) provides the percentage of *P. falciparum* vs *P. vivax* and ovale as well as current information on resistance to chloroquine for each country.

PLAGUE — is caused by a bacteria that infects wild rodents in many parts of the world, including the western United States and parts of South America, Africa, and Asia. Epidemics occur when domestic rats become infected and spread the disease to man. Bubonic plague is transmitted by infected fleas, while pneumonic plague is spread directly to other people by coughing. Plague is accompanied by fever, enlarged lymph nodes (bubonic plague) and less commonly pneumonia (pneumonic plague).

Treatment is with doxycycline 100 mg twice daily. Treat fever as necessary. Isolate patient, particularly if coughing. Drainage of abscesses (buboes) may be necessary (see page 96). Exposed persons should be watched for 10 days, but incubation is usually 2 to 6 days. Only travelers to Vietnam, Cambodia, and Laos are at enough risk to consider using plague vaccine, unless a local epidemic has broken out (see Appendix A).

YELLOW FEVER — An arbovirus, this disease is found in tropical areas of South and Central America and Africa. This viral disease is contracted by the bite of the *Aedes aegypti* mosquito (and others) 2 weeks previously. Onset is sudden with a fever of 102 to 104 degrees. The pulse is usually rapid the first day, but becomes slow by the second day. In mild cases the fever falls by crises 2 to 5 days after onset. This remission lasts for hours to several days. Next the fever returns, but the pulse remains slow. Jaundice, vomiting of black blood, and severe loss of protein in the urine (causing it to become foamy) occurs during this stage. Hemorrhages may be noted in the mouth and skin (petechiae). The patient is confused and senses are dulled. Delirium, convulsions and coma occur at death in approximately 10% of cases. If the patient is to survive, this last febrile episode lasts from 3 to 9 days. With remission the patient is well, with no after effects from the disease. Immunization is available and required for travel to many countries (see Appendix A).

LYME DISEASE — is caused by a spirochete, Borrelia burgdorferi. The disease lives in various mammals, but is transmitted to humans by the bite of several species of ticks. The disease is most common in the Northeast, extending through Connecticut and Massachusetts down to Maryland; in Wisconsin and Minnesota; throughout the states of California and Oregon; and in parts of California and Utah. It has also been found in various south Atlantic and south central states, and in several European countries. The disease goes through several phases. In Stage 1, after an incubation of 3 days to a month, from 30% to 80% of victims develop a circular lesion in the area of the bite. It has a clear center, raised border, is painless, and ranges from 1 to 23 inches in diameter. There are usually several such patches. The patient feels lethargy, has headache, muscle and joint pain, and enlarged lymph nodes. In stage 2 10% to 15% of patient can develop a meningitis, fewer than 10% heart problems. Symptoms may last for months, but are generally self-limited. Approximately 60% enter stage 3 - the development of actual arthritis. Frequently a knee is involved. The swelling can be impressive. Stage 3 can start abruptly several weeks to 2 years after the onset of the initial rash. Treatment of Stage 1 Lyme disease is tetracycline, such as doxycycline 100 mg taken twice daily for 10 to 20 days. Alternate drugs are penicillin and erythromycin. Treatment of choice for stage 2 and 3 Lyme disease consists of high doses of injectable penicillin G (20 million units intravenously daily for 10 days).

APPENDIX A

IMMUNIZATION SCHEDULES

Immunization schedules for domestic and foreign travel are listed below. Further information can be obtained from a booklet titled, *Health Information for International Travel*, U.S. Public Health Service, Superintendent of Documents, U.S. Government Printing Office, Washington, D.C. 20402 ($2.50 includes postage). An excellent book for foreign travel is *Traveling Well* by Dr W. Scott Harkonen (Dodd, Mead. $11.95 paperback).

Due to the rapidly changing international requirements, it would be advisable to contact one of several services that can provide updated disease activity and suggested/recommended immunization requirements on a country by country basis. For a small donation ($25 is recommended) IAMAT (International Association for Medical Assistance to Travelers) will send a yearly updated schedule of country immunization information, list of English speaking doctors, and climate charts. Their address is 417 Center Street, Lewiston, NY 14092. For a $10.00 per country charge, Herchmer Medical Group will provide a recommended immunization schedule that includes current information on disease activity, US State Department Travel Advisories from a database that is updated weekly. Contact Herchmer Medical Group Ltd, 109 East 89th Avenue, Merrillville, IN 46410 (Telephone 219 769-0866).

The 20 most commonly required immunizations are listed below. Some of these schedules do not provide total protection, but they will then frequently ameliorate the disease. Prevention is a lot safer and less traumatic than attempting to cure a patient.

CHOLERA — Primary immunization consists of two doses given subcutaneous or intramuscular 1 week to 1 month or more apart. Booster injections are required ever 6 months. Dosages are: children 6 months to 5 years, 0.2ml; 5 to 10 years, 0.3 ml; over 10 years, 0.5 ml. This immunization provides 60 to 80% protection — if obvious exposure occurs, prompt prophylaxis with doxycycline 100 mg, 1 tablet daily, may prevent infection. Immunization is effective 6 days after receiving injection, immediately, if booster.

HEPATITIS A (Infectious Hepatitis) — A single does of pooled immune globulin (10% solution) protects against or modifies this form of hepatitis which is commonly caught from tainted food or water supplies. It must not be given at the same times as the Measles, Mumps, Rubella (MMR) vaccine. It may be given at least 14 days before MMR or 6 months after MMR. There are no apparent problems in the administration of Oral Polio Vaccine or Yellow Fever vaccine with or near immune globulin administration. Dosage depends upon body weight and length of time of required protection. At maximal doses it still must be repeated every 6 months for continued protection.

Immune Globulin Dosage*

weight	short term (3 months)	long term (3 months)	
50 pounds	0.5 ml	1.0 ml	(repeat
50-100 pounds	1.0 ml	2.5 ml	every
100 pounds	2.0 ml	5.0 ml	6 mos.)

*Also called immune serum globulin and gamma globulin.

HEPATITIS B (Serum Hepatitis) — Most commonly spread by hypodermic usage, sexual contact, blood transfusions. This disease has a very high prevalence in many areas of the world. Immunization is from 1.0 ml IM injections of Heptavax-B vaccine given on day 0, 1 month, and 6 months. Wholesale cost as of August 1987 is about $160.00 for 1 full course of immunization. Duration of protection and need for revaccination has not been defined. A blood test to determine resistance can be performed. If the antibody level falls below 10 SRUs, revaccination should be considered. The injection must be given in the deltoid muscle.

JAPANESE ENCEPHALITIS — Immunization requires 3 doses to be given at weekly intervals, with a booster dose at 12 to 18 months and at 4 year intervals thereafter if risk continues. This vaccine is not made in the US. The location of a JE vaccination center in the US may be obtained by calling the CDC, Fort Collins (303-221-6429).

INFLUENZA — Vaccines are prepared that give 1 to 2 years of immunity for prevalent strains of influenza A or B. New strains are constantly arising that require formulation of new vaccines to compensate for this "antigenic drift." Dosage is 0.5 ml IM in the deltoid muscle, given in the fall of the year. Not required for routine expedition work, unless heading into an epidemic area.

MALARIA — No vaccine is currently available. See page 128.

MEASLES, MUMPS, RUBELLA — One 0.5 ml dose given subcutaneously should provide life long immunity. The MMR vaccine provides adequate protection against all three viral diseases, but each vaccine is available separately. May not be given if allergic to eggs or neomycin. Must be given at least 14 days prior to or 6 weeks to 3 months after immune serum globulin.

MENINGOCOCCAL — This vaccine need be used only under special circumstances (military personnel in the U.S. and persons traveling to areas of the world where meningococcal infection is epidemic). The A/C/Y/W135 vaccine by Squibb-Connaught is given 0.5 ml subcutaneously. Duration of protection is unknown, but appears to be at least 3 years in those over 4 years of age.

PLAGUE — In most countries of Africa, Asia and the Americas where plague is reported, the risk of exposure exists primarily in rural mountainous or upland areas. Adult immunization consists of 3 injections of 0.5 ml, 0.5 ml, and 0.2 ml (in that order) about 4 weeks apart and two boosters of 0.2 ml 6 months apart, then 1 dose ever 1 to 2 years if needed.

PNEUMOCOCCUS — A vaccine against streptococcal (formerly called pneumococcal) pneumonia has been developed for high risk patients with chronic diseases or respiratory problems. One 0.5 ml IM injection in the deltoid muscle probably provides a life-long immunity.

POLIOMYELITIS — Trivalent oral polio vaccine (OPV) is the vaccine of choice for all infants, children, and adolescents (up to 18th birthday). The primary series is 3 doses, with dose 2 given at least 6 weeks after 1 and dose 3 given 8 — 12 months after dose 2. The supplemental dose is given to children at age 4 to 6 years. Anyone having a partial series may continue with the next dose(s), regardless of how long before the last dose was given.

Areas of increased risk include Mexico, Central America and South America. Prior to travel to these areas, anyone who has completed the primary OPV series in the past should be given a single additional dose of OPV. Unimmunized adults should be given the four full dose series of injectable inactivated polio vaccine (IPV) (3 doses given at 1 to 2 month intervals, followed by a 4th dose 6 to 12 months after the 3rd dose), if time allows or a minimum of 2 doses of IPV given a month apart. If less than a month remains prior to departure, the administration of a single dose of OPV may be justified due to potential high risk of exposure to wild poliovirus and the more rapid protective effect of OPV.

RABIES — A pre-exposure regimen of rabies vaccine is appropriate for persons routinely exposed to potential rabid animals - including skunks, fox, raccoon and bats. It does not eliminate the need for additional therapy after rabies exposure, but simplifies post-exposure therapy by eliminating the requirement for rabies immune globulin (RIG) and by decreasing the number of doses of vaccine required. Prevention with human diploid cell vaccine (HDCV) is 3 doses given 1.0 ml IM in the deltoid muscle on days 0, 7, and 28.

Post-exposure immunization for those previously immunized is 2 doses on days 0 and 3, with no RIG. If no prior immunization, give RIG 20 IU/kg (1/2 in bite site and 1/2 IM) and 5 doses of HDCV on days 0, 3, 7, 14, and 28. See also page 98.

ROCKY MOUNTAIN SPOTTED FEVER
TICK FEVER; TICK TYPHUS - England
FIEBRE MANCHODA - Mexico
FIEBRE PETEQUIAL - Colombia
FIEBRE MACULOSA - Brazil
— This disease is spread by ticks with cases being reported from 47 states in the U.S. Most of these cases are from the states of North Carolina, Virginia, Maryland, the Rocky Mountain states and the state of Washington. The vaccine for this disease has been removed from the market, but prevention by use of insect repellent and frequent tick removal checks is effective. See also page 124.

SMALLPOX — This disease has been declared eradicated by the World Health Organization in May 1980. A vaccine is available only to military and laboratory personnel working with this virus.

TETANUS — DIPHTHERIA — Officially, all persons should have a tetanus booster every 10 years; 5 years for puncture wounds, bites, and other contaminated wounds. Because of this, any trip member should have a booster so recent as to be no older than 5 years before the calculated return date of the trip. This alters the official recommendation considerably, but precludes requiring booster shots in the field or emergency protection with tetanus immune globulin. Dosage is 0.5 ml of dT vaccine given IM.

TYPHOID — Immunization should be completed before heading into areas where typhoid fever is known to be epidemic (many countries of Africa, Asia, and Central and South America). The vaccine is from 70% to 90% effective in preventing the disease and also decreases the severity of the disease. Immunization consists of two 0.5 ml doses given 1 month apart, with a booster dose every 3 years.

TYPHUS — A disease spread worldwide, it is prevented by eliminating lice. Production of the vaccine in the US has been discontinued and there are no plans for commercial production of new vaccine. No typhus cases are known to have occurred in an American traveler since 1950. This disease is frequent after major disasters; approximately 3 million people died of it during World War II.

YELLOW FEVER — Immunization is required for travel to many countries in South America, Africa and Asia. The immunization consists of one 0.5 ml injection, which confers immunity for 10 years. It is available only at designated Yellow Fever Vaccination Centers (check your local health department for the nearest facility).

APPENDIX B

READING LIST

In the last 10 years there has been a virtual explosion of literature directed towards the mountain climber, foreign traveler, and others in pursuit of wilderness adventure. Articles in medical journals add to this literature on a monthly basis. The following books and sources of information, while certainly not exhaustive, are valuable additions to this literature:

Auerbach, Paul, MD: *Medicine for the Outdoors*, Little, Brown, Boston, 1986. 347 pages. An extensive discussion of outdoor related medical problems written for the layman.

Auerbach, Paul, MD and Geehr, Edward, MD (ed): *Management of Wilderness and Environmental Emergencies*, Macmillan, New York, 1983. 656 pages. An extensive discussion of outdoor related medical problems written for the physician. An expensive book, but a valuable reference work.

Breyfogle, Newell: *The Common Sense Medical Guide and Outdoor Reference*, McGraw-Hill, New York, 1981. 413 pages. Considerable input from outdoor recreation specialists make this a valuable book for outdoor youth group leaders. Contains emergency camping and survival tips, as well as home and vehicle disaster information.

Buttaravoli, Philip, MD, and Stair, Thomas, MD: *Common Simple Emergencies*, Brady Communications Company, Inc, Bowie, Maryland, 1985. 306 pages. Designed for the emergency room physician, many practical advanced first aid techniques are well described.

Harkonen, W. Scott, MD: *Traveling Well*, Dodd, Mead, New York, 1984. 286 pages. Must reading for those contemplating travel outside of the United States.

Kodet, E. Russel, MD, and Angier, Bradford: *Being Your Own Wilderness Doctor*, Stackpole, Harrisburg, PA, 1968. 127 pages. A classic, one of the best books written for the layman on emergency care in the outdoors.

Nelson, Richard, MD et al: *Environmental Emergencies*, W.B. Saunders, Philadelphia, 1985. 359 pages. A very compact book, written for physicians, with extensive descriptions and concise treatment plans. A must book for every physician interested in outdoor medical problems.

Pozos, Robert, and Born, David: *Hypothermia*, New Century Publishers, Piscataway, NJ, 1982. 173 pages. A nationally recognized work that is designed for layman.

Ramamurti, C.P., MD and Tinker, Richard, MD: *Orthopaedics in Primary Care*, Williams & Wilkins, Baltimore, 1979. 385 pages. An excellent book written for the non-orthopedic physician.

Wesley, John: *Primitive Physick*, R. Hawes, London, 1755. 142 pages. An historic self care medical manual written by the founder of the Methodist church, in popular use during pre-colonial times in frontier America. The epigraph of this book comes from his first chapter.

Wilkerson, James, MD (Ed): *Medicine for Mountaineering*, 3rd Edition, Mountaineers, Seattle, 1985. 438 pages. Provides information concerning advanced medical care of serious outdoor injuries. A must book for every outdoor traveler's library.

Wilkerson, James, MD (Ed): *Hypothermia, Frostbite and other Cold Injuries*, Mountaineers, Seattle, 1986. 105 pages. Important information about this critical subject.

Also by Doctor Forgey:

Hypothermia: Death by Exposure, ICS Books, Merrillville, IN, 1985. 185 pages. A study of the most dangerous risk that the outdoor traveler will experience. While written for the layman, it contains a section for paramedical personnel and physicians on pre- and post-hospital management of chronic and immersion hypothermic victims. $9.95.

Campfire Stories: Things that go bump in the night, ICS Books, Merrillville, IN, 1985. 20 scary stories that have been selected for their ease in telling around the campfire. $9.95.

INSTANT REFERENCE CLINICAL INDEX

Rapidly look up your problem here!

Symptoms, regional anatomical or organ system involvement, therapy, diseases and traumatic conditions by common and scientific name, and medications by brand and generic name are listed and cross-referenced.

Page numbers in **bold** refer to principle listings.